BUILDING **COMPREHENSION** AND **LITERACY** SKILLS IN GLOBAL BLACK HISTORY FOR HIGH SCHOOLERS

KADEEN DOBBS

COPYRIGHT & CREDITS

BUILDING **COMPREHENSION** AND **LITERACY** SKILLS IN GLOBAL BLACK HISTORY FOR HIGH SCHOOLERS

ISBN: 978-976-655-123-0

Illustrations: Karlashay Wilson

Book Cover Design: Andre Rankine

Editing & Formatting : The Publisher's Notebook Limited

TABLE OF CONTENTS

THE TRANSFORMATIONAL LEADER'S AFFIRMATIONS i

INTRODUCTION II

The AFRICAN DNA IS US II

A GLIMPSE OF OUR AFRICAN ANCESTRY-SELF- IDENTITY 1

Context Clues - Africa, The Land of Kings and Queens 1

Rhetorical Question / Pun - The Origin of Black Hairdos 9

Recognizing Problem and Solution - Grooming Afro-Textured Hair 20

Distinguishing Fact From Opinion - The Beginning of Racial Segregation and Inequality 27

Literary Genres - How "They" Turned Us Against Each Other 31

Visualization - The Power of the Black DNA 36

Self-Questioning - Why Jesus Could NEVER be white 42

Determining Importance / Synthesizing - Black Worship 53

POST SLAVERY... 59

Bias And Perspective - The Dress Code That Embraced Decolonization 59

Flashback 63

Madame C.J. Walker, From Poverty to Affluence 65

Cause And Effect - Black Wall Street 70

Making Inferences - Strange Fruit Hanging From A Tree 76

Tone : Malcokm X 81

Mood : Dr. Martin Luther King Jr. 85

Compare and Contrast 88

Sequencing Events : Marcus Garvey 95
The Author's Purpose - Black Inventors 99
Identifying Themes : Nelson Mandela 107
Figurative Language - The WAY 110
Paraphrasing - Bob Marley 115
Summarizing : Claudine Gay 121
7 JAMAICANS THAT MADE THEIR MARK IN BLACK AMERICAN HISTORY 127
Recognizing Character Traits : Colin Powell 127
Identifying The Flashback Technique : Angella Reid 131
Angella Reid, Lady Extraordinaire 131
Comprehending Chronological Order -: Lester Holt 135
Making Connections- Text- To- Self : Maurice Ashley 139
Focusing on Text-To-World : Clive Campbell 143
Types of Characters : Bessie Stringfield 151
Foreshadowing : Sheryl Lee Ralph 155
KNOWLEDGE APPLIED IS POWER! 159
Analyzing - What "Truly" Makes You Jamaican 159
Identifying Point of View (POV) : Althea Laing 165
Text -To- Text : Usain Bolt 171
Predicting Outcomes : The Jamaican Bobsled Team 177
Transitions : Mae Jemison 181
Listening Comprehension : Dr Gladys West 185
Writing a Biography Report : William Robinson Clarke 188
Reading Techniques- Skimming and Scanning : Jerry Lawson 193

Using Project Based Learning to build comprehension, literacy and research skills. 196

THE TEACHER'S GUIDE - GOALS AND OBJECTIVES **199**

INTRODUCTION 199

THE INTERDISCIPLINARY CURRICULUM approach and design to increase COMPREHENSION, LITERACY and RESEARCH skills in GLOBAL BLACK HISTORY 202

DISCIPLINE: Religious Education 206

DISCIPLINE: Civics 207

DISCIPLINE: History and Geography 208

DISCIPLINE: Social Studies- Social Skills, Ethics, Philosophy, Psychology and Anthropology Perspective for Social -Emotional Development. 210

DISCIPLINE: Social Studies- Global Connections 212

DISCIPLINE: English Language and English Literature 213

DISCIPLINE: Literacy 215

Summary 217

ABOUT THE AUTHOR 219

REFERENCES 220

BUILDING COMPREHENSION AND LITERACY SKILLS IN GLOBAL BLACK HISTORY FOR HIGH SCHOOLERS
Written by
Kadeen Dobbs

The Transformational Leader's Affirmations

I am powerful

I am a visionary

I solve problems

I invent

If it has never been done before

I will do it

I am a nation builder

I am not limited by my circumstances

Instead, I soar over every obstacle

I am focused

I have dominion over the Earth through Christ Jesus

The world is a better place because I add, create and innovate

I positively transform

I lead

I am a transformational leader!

INTRODUCTION

THE AFRICAN DNA IS US

The African DNA began, of course, on the continent of Africa. When Africans were captured or sold and enslaved by the whites they were transported to, and sold in the Caribbean, the Americas and Europe. That African DNA courses through our veins and though intermarriages and interracial relationships have unfolded, some consensual, while far too many were not, out of this ethnicity mixture, came the birth of our motto, "Out of many, One People."

Though scattered across the globe, we are connected by our ancestry, our illustrious beginning, in Africa. Hence, the relevance of Global Black History. We share a past of slavery that has divided and separated us by oceans, distance, but still we have remained connected by similar experiences and circumstances. It is a circumstance that has chained us to shackles for almost 400 years, and though freedom has rung its prolonged reverberations, the mental and spiritual ramifications still rear its grotesque, diabolical head. There is a resounding rhetorical question that has never truly been adequately answered: who are we?

African families were scattered across the globe, never to see each other again, but our roots connected us. Greed and oppression could not stop our rising and the emancipation of progress resounded this undeniable truth, "Yes, we can and we have."

Our forefathers were forcibly brought to the New World by white merchants, traders who perceived black bodies as goods, and so our ancestors were sold across the globe. Slavery in Jamaica lasted for over 200 years. The majority of slaves who were brought here by ships came from Ghana, Nigeria and Central Africa. This included individuals from the Akan, Ashanti, Yoruba, Ibo and Ibibio tribes (Embassy of Jamaica, 2007) Today, the Maroons carry out their ancestors, the West Africans' culture, in the hills where they have withdrawn to live, or in the communities they have established. Despite all slaves coming from

Africa, they all had different religions varying from Muslim, to Islam but the majority were animistic. They used bones, feathers, rituals and incantations and believed inanimate objects had characteristics and qualities of living things. It is believed that "animism, is the belief in innumerable spiritual beings concerned with human affairs and capable of helping or harming human interests." (Park, 2023). Hence, they worshipped objects, gods carved out of wood and stone and recognized them as their deities. They had a belief in "innumerable spiritual beings." The missionaries introduced the Christian faith to both the slaves and the plantation owners in Jamaica, because when the British came and saw plantation owners' behavior towards the slaves, they were appalled because it was anything but "Christian like."

However, in Africa, there were people who practiced the Christian faith, but it was referred to as "The Way" after the crucifixion of Jesus Christ. God is known as YHWH (Yahweh) and in the Old Testament, the Israelites just knew there was one true and living God and so the universe must not be worshipped. Thus, they worshipped not creation, but rather the Creator of ALL creation. Their faith had no name, it just was. Then Christ came on the scene in the New Testament and there existed no more need for blood sacrifices. Christianity was in Africa before the Europeans arrived. Saul, the Roman, stopped persecuting Christians (believers, saints, followers of Christ as they are referred to in the Bible) because he had an encounter with Christ on the Damascus Road. Romans became Christians and Constantine made it even more popular by legalizing it. Nero was one that hated Christians. He was a Roman who used his colosseum as a place of entertainment to burn Christians alive. Christianity is not a white man's religion. Focus on CHRIST in Christianity. Follow Christ, not religion. Religious rituals provide no peace, but a real, authentic, true relationship with Jesus (The Messiah) does. This workbook does NOT support the following perceptions:

- ONLY black people will go to heaven. On the contrary, salvation is for ALL, regardless of skin colour, race, ethnicity and socio- economic status.
- Racism- God is LOVE and he instructs us to love ALL and forgive.
- Other races are inferior- God created ALL and heaven will reflect God's creation which is a kaleidoscope of shades, shapes and personalities.

What happened to slaves in Jamaica is not unique to this region and its people. This diaspora of injustice has happened to every slave in the world: oppression, separation, mutilation, rape, beatings, murder and unspoken inhumane atrocities too vile to be uttered, but etched in history, our past. The fight for true freedom after the abolishment of slavery was happening in every area across the world that once had slaves as free workers.

The movement for civil rights as a black person was global. There was social unrest after the abolishment of slavery, not just in Jamaica.

However, this workbook aims to not just focus on slavery but rather shed light on influential black leaders, black inventors, and black movements that shaped our free global future. Light must also dawn on what the African civilization was like before white merchants arrived.

Additionally, literacy skills will improve when it is centred around "our history" as opposed to unknown texts, stories and a genre that is unfamiliar and thus unrelatable. The relatability, of content increases interests, thus engagement and understanding and the self- motivation to read and research.

Know your past, and so no longer stand divided and be in enmity with your fellow black brothers and sisters.

Our history is global and requires an integration for a deeper appreciation and understanding of who we are as a Jamaican nation in a global community. More power to our black children!

Let the learning begin! -An individual who reads to learn must always take the **INITIATIVE** to find out unknown information in a text that has been read.

Questions:

- Who was Constantine?
- Who was Nero?
- Do you know of any Maroon communities that are in Jamaica?

Do the research.

A GLIMPSE OF OUR AFRICAN ANCESTRY-SELF- IDENTITY

Wall paintings from King Tutankhamun's tomb, showing the umber skin tone of ancient Egyptians, courtesy of the Smithsonian. *(Retrieved from https://www.thecollector.com/were-ancient-egyptians-black/)*

CONTEXT CLUES - AFRICA, THE LAND OF KINGS AND QUEENS

These are hints/clues provided by the author to help readers to find out the meaning of a word without using the dictionary. The reader will have to rely on information surrounding the unknown, difficult or unusual word(s) to decipher or figure out its meaning. There are different types of context clues that can help us to figure out the meaning of an unknown word. They are:

Context Clues by Definition/Explanation- The unknown word is defined, or its meaning is given.

Context Clues by Antonym- The unfamiliar word is understood by providing its opposite or making a contrast.

Context Clues by Synonym- The clue/hint for the meaning of the word is provided by giving a word that is same or similar in meaning to the difficult word.

Africa, The Land of Kings and Queens

Before our ancestors were enslaved we were kings, queens, emperors, empresses, pharaohs- rulers of ancient Egypt, monarchs and we sat on our thrones in Africa, ruling with power, strength and dignity. We were wealthy, rich in gold and silver.

The whites did not arrive in Africa finding an uncivilized nation and people. Yes, our culture was different but on the contrary, we were proud, fearless, prosperous, educated and advanced.

Queen Nefertiti of ancient Egypt (1353-1336 BC) was the wife of King Akhenaton. Historians described her as black and beautiful, and she and her husband are credited for influencing the practice of monotheism which is the practice of worshipping one god. They worshipped the god Atken. The Egyptians were known for worshipping many gods, which was known as polytheism. When Queen Nefertiti's mummy was unearthed she was in excellent condition with her dark skin. Wall paintings from King Tutankhamun's (King Tut) tomb show the umber (dark brown) skin tone of ancient Egyptians. (Lesso,2022)

Africa has many tribes and languages. The Lemba, the Black Jews of Southern Africa, follow the Jewish rituals and they speak the Bantu language. This is a group of people who currently reside in Africa. This was the startling discovery that one doctor unearthed when he took DNA samples from the men of this tribe. Doctor David Goldstein observed that the Lemba's Y chromosome has ancestral connection to past Judaic populations. King Solomon of the Bible was King of a unified Hebrew nation, Judah and Israel. Now what the doctor did was he and his team collected DNA samples from males from the Bantu tribe (Africa), Yemeni (Arab) and Sephardic and Ashkenazi Jews. The DNA results showed two things:

- All three clans had the same past paternal ancestry and

- Within the Lemba tribe, these Y chromosomes show that the leaders of the past played a role in bringing the Lemba tribe out of Israel (Lost Tribes of Israel, 2000)

Israel is in the Middle East. The practices that the Lemba tribe followed were Semitic, not African. Semitic is a family of languages that includes Hebrew, Arabic, Aramaic and other ancient languages. Aramaic is the language that

Jesus spoke. It is an Afro- Asiatic family (Oxford Languages, 2023). This group like The Hebrews of the Bible refused to intermarry. Doctor Goldstein stated:

“We know for instance that there was no white or Jewish penetration of Africa until very recent times.” (Lost Tribes of Israel, 2000).

Let us dissect this bible story and demonstrate how science supports scripture. Queen Sheba had been impressed by Solomon’s wisdom for he answered all of her challenging questions with such intellect, wisdom, knowledge and understanding. His insight was astounding and captivating. In 1 Kings 10:10 it is written:

“Never again were so many spices brought in as those that Queen of Sheba gave to Solomon.”

Queen Sheba had to declare:

“In wisdom and wealth, you have far exceeded the report I have heard.” (1 Kings 10:6-KJV)

The story of King Solomon and the Queen of Sheba from Ethiopia can be read in the books of the Holy Bible, specifically, the books of Kings and Chronicles. The queen of Sheba travelled to Israel bringing gold, jewels and spices. She was a lover of knowledge and so sought out King Solomon who, according to scripture, was the wisest man that ever lived. However, before the conversation unfolds between King Solomon and Queen of Sheba, there is a black character who makes a statement. 1 Solomon 1:5 reads:

“I am black and comely.”

The woman who made this statement was a Shulamite and she was the first bride of Solomon. As the scriptures continue, she remarks that she is deeply tanned because she works in the vineyard, but regardless she is of a dark complexion (black). She feels embarrassment because of her skin tone, but Solomon considers her beautiful and marries her.

In Solomon 5:11, the Shulamite woman (bride) praises Solomon (her beloved) and she states:

His head is as the most fine gold; his locks are bushy and black as a raven (KJ21)

Note the description of Solomon’s hair.

As we read the story of King Solomon and the Queen of Sheba, along with the evidence provided by Doctor Goldstein, we see why the original Israelites or Hebrews are believed to be have been black and thus the current Israelites residing in Israel are immigrants. When the Babylonians attacked Jerusalem in Israel, the original Hebrews fled to Africa, where they reside today. Some were taken into exile or captivity to Babylon (See 2 Kings 24:14, Ezra 5:12, Jeremiah 25:4- 9 for reference). The Babylonians destroyed the temple that Solomon had built, and many rich, educated and powerful families were taken captive and the ten tribes of Israel were scattered.

Queen Cleopatra's story is one that has often graced the screen. The first Cleopatra movie was produced in 1934, by Paramount Pictures. Since then, Netflix, documentaries and animated films have been created to narrate her biography. She was known for her beauty and her intellect and historians believe that her beautiful, soft and glowing skin was due to her frequent "milk baths." It was customary for Egyptian queens or women of royal breeding to do this to improve the overall appearance and texture of their skin.

Queen Cleopatra was born into royalty in Egypt. She is remembered for her love affairs with Mark Antony and Julius Caesar. She became a queen at eighteen after her father's death; and she was a strong and sharp ruler. Historically, it is recorded that she invited Julius Caesar on a voyage with her up the River Nile. This is the same river that Moses was rescued from by Pharaoh's daughter, who raised him as her son. This is evident in Exodus 2:5. As Queen Cleopatra's skin tone has not been conclusively determined by historians, there is much debate to this day as to what her colour truly was. However, here is evidence to support that Moses was black.

Something to ponder. If Moses the Hebrew, had been white, how would Pharaoh's daughter have been able to hide him for forty years among black-skinned Egyptians? Pharaoh had given the decree to kill all Hebrew males. Do you think he would have allowed one to live under his roof after giving such a decree?

Moses did not look out of place in the Egyptian household because they all had the same skin tone. Let us analyze Exodus 4:5-6:

6 And the Lord said furthermore unto him, **Put now thine hand into thy bosom.** And he put his hand into his bosom: and **when he took it out, behold, his hand was leprous as snow.**

7 And he said, **Put thine hand into thy bosom again**. And he put his hand into

his bosom again; and plucked it out of his bosom, and, behold, **it was turned again as his other flesh**. (KJV)

What colour is snow? White. Moses was not white.

In the Book of Numbers, chapter 12, it is written that Miriam and Aaron were not pleased with Moses' choice for a wife. She was a Kushite an Ethiopian of a dark-skinned tone, but her skin tone was not the problem; it was because she was not a Hebrew, an Israelite like them. They began to complain and grumble that perhaps Moses was not really hearing from God and that Moses was not the only one to whom God could give instructions. God heard the murmuring of course, and Miriam was struck with leprosy that made her as white as snow. Leprosy in the Bible is described as white. Moses a black man married a black Ethiopian woman, and so what colour would be their children?

Now let us discuss another black King. King Shaka Zulu is the son of an exiled princess. He was a warrior who was raised by his mother. She was Princess Nandi. When his father died, he became chief of the Zulu people. He was strong and brutal and whoever disobeyed him was killed. When his mother died, he ordered around seven thousand people to be killed for he felt they were not sorrowful enough. He went barefoot, and he forced his soldiers to do the same. He wanted their feet to toughen up and make them more agile in a fight. Men could not marry until they proved themselves worthy in a battle. He was assassinated in 1828. He was forty-one years old. King Zulu was buried in an unmarked grave. (Ducksters, 2022)

Africa, the continent of kings and queens, and the place to which the Hebrew Israelites fled. This is our heritage, our history one of royalty and intrigue.

1. **Identify and write two (2) types of context clues used in the passage.**

____

____

____

____

2. Explain the following remark. Who is the speaker? Why was such a comment made?

"In wisdom and wealth, you have far exceeded the report I have heard."

3. Paraphrase the 4th paragraph. Make every effort not to exceed three sentences.

4. What new information has been presented to you?

5. How will this new information be beneficial or useful to you?

6. What active ingredient is present in milk that will make the skin soft, beautiful and glowing?

7. Extract the main idea from each paragraph. Include ONLY the relevant supporting details for each main idea. Condense to one paragraph and omit quotes and examples (80-100 words).

8. Find the nation of Israel on the World Map. There are four seas. Name each.

9. Which body of water is to the west of Israel?

10. Look at the World Map and speculate/hypothesize or give an approximate route by boat for the following:

a. The journey or travel route by boat from Africa to Israel.

b. Similarly, the journey or travel route by boat from Egypt to Israel.

Please note that the landscape or topography have changed by both natural occurrences and interferences with man's demarcation of land and renaming of places.

RHETORICAL QUESTION / PUN - THE ORIGIN OF BLACK HAIRDOS

Rhetorical Question: This is a question that does not require a response. The objective is to get you to think and to rouse deep introspection.

Pun- A pun is a literary device that uses witty, clever language within a sentence to convey a different meaning. It is supposed to be humorous. The intention is to make the reader laugh as figurative language, whether it be a word or phrase, teases the thought process to look at the "word/s" and think differently about the situation proposed in the text.

Vocabulary Building- Cultural Appropriation- Cultural appropriation is when members of a majority group adopt cultural elements of a minority group in an exploitative, disrespectful, or stereotypical way. (Britannica, 2023). A minority group is subordinate to a more dominant group. They do not possess as much power.

When the adoption or imitation of such cultural elements occur, the minority group is not acknowledged, recognized or appreciated.

African Hairstyles- The Origin of Black Hair Hairdos.

Indira Arie sings:

"I am not my hair. I am not this skin. I am the soul that lives within."

Is this just catchy lyrics or is there really some truth to it? Am I not defined by my hair or my skin tone? Doesn't society judge us based on our looks? Aren't first impressions lasting? Isn't straight hair more acceptable than an afro?

The manner in which we groom our hair has African roots. Here are some hairstyles that are popular in black culture that has its "roots" (pun intended) in Africa. Black hairstyles can be found in drawings, engravings and hieroglyphics from Ancient Egypt.

Standard English	*Patois/Dialect*
Wigs	**False hair**

When Queen Nefertiti was discovered in 1913, she was showcasing a towering hairstyle. Headdresses and wigs within the Egyptian culture were symbolic of one's rank and was essential to royal and wealthy males and females alike. In 2050 BC (Before Christ) wigs were created with a thick skullcap. Attached to the skullcap was human hair, wool, palm fibers and other materials. Slaves and servants were forbidden to wear wigs. This was the Egyptian law. (Horne, 2019).

Standard English	*Patois/Dialect*
Twisted locks	**Rasta**

Dreadlocks have been perceived as a hairstyle connected with the 20th century Jamaica and Rastafarianism culture, but its origins go beyond that as this hairstyle is seen in the Bible written over two thousand years ago. Rastafarians in Jamaica follow the teachings of the Ethiopian Emperor, Ras Tafari, Haile Selassie.

Samson of the Bible had made a Nazirite vow which was never to cut his hair. This was the secret to Samson's strength. The Rastafarians have also taken this vow.

In the book of Judges:

"Delilah lulled Samson to sleep in her lap and then called a man, who cut off Samson's seven locks of hair." (Judges, 16:19-ESV) Samson was an Israelite, from the Dan tribe.

However, the history of dreadlocks has been dated back to 500 BCE (Before Christian Era) in Africa. Due to the nature of African hair, historians believe that this hairstyle has been around long before that. Does this not prove the Bible? History supports the Bible. Dreadlocks have also been worn by Africans in Kenya, Tanzania, Nigeria and Ghana. Mummies excavated from Egyptian tombs by archaeologists are found sporting hairstyles that look like dreadlocks. Is this not absolutely remarkable?

Do you know where dreadlocks are currently trending? Japan. Some Japanese men admire black dancers, are hip hop fans and admire the black culture. Additionally, Japanese rappers sport dreadlocks. However, Japanese men speak about not being able to get a corporate job while sporting such a hairdo. They also face criticism as individuals perceive the hairstyle as unsanitary. For some, the love for reggae and the "rasta" roots will make them continue sporting dreadlocks. For some men, who sport dreadlocks in Japan, they love standing out and the attention they may get from tourists and the ladies. Is this appropriation or appreciation?

Standard English	*Patois/Dialect*
Bantu Knots	**Chiney Bumps**

Bantu Knots has its roots in Africa. Bantu means "people" among many African languages. This is a representation of over four hundred different groups in Africa. These knots are also known as Zulu knots. This is so because the Zulu people of South Africa, a Bantu ethnic group originated the hairstyle. Nubian knots is another name.

This hairstyle caused quite an uproar of disapproval when it was worn by Joan Andrea Hutchinson on television. The year was 1996. She was hosting a TV programme and these were some of the comments made by the viewers:

"Teck dat dutty bumpyhead gyal off di TV / tck dat rasta looking gyal off di TV/ If my maid came to work looking like you I would send her home / you are a damn disgrace to women / you are like dirt." (Hutchinson, 2021)

However, Joan Andrea Hutchinson is a confident, black woman and in 2018, when she received the Order of Distinction, she wore her Nubian knots to collect her award. The Order of Distinction is given to any Jamaican citizen that has given significant and outstanding service to the country. It can also be given to an Honorary member. Honorary members are not Jamaican citizens, but have contributed significantly to the country.

Read Hutchinson's iconic clapback poem to the prejudiced comments she received in 1996.

Retrieved from https://jamaicans.com/they-thought-they-hurt-by-saying-teck-dat-dutty-bumpyhead-gyal-off-di-tv/

Dat Bumpy Head Gyal

Tell mi say mi no good enough fi you TV screen

How mi offend you eyesight

Tell mi say mi is a black, ugly, bumpyhead gal

And mi tell you, mi feeling right

Cuss mi say mi is a bootoo, and mi no have no class
Trace mi and galang rude
Tell mi say a educated woman shoulda know better
And I tell you mi feeling good

You say mi hairstyle disgusting chaka chaka an tan bad
And favour like something out a street
And say mi should a shame fi lef mi house tan so
And mi smile, for mi feeing sweet

You see, the truth is, mi not ashamed of mi owna self
Mi not afraid of me
When mi look into the mirror, mi like the somebody
Weh mi see a look pon me

Mi like her thick nappy hair and her broad face
Mi like her in and out of clothes
But most of all mi love weh she stan up for and defend
And, a no pose she a pose

But serious, when you a go fall in love with you
And leggo of all you fear
When you ago take the time tell God thanks fi you life
Instead of fret bout 'hair'

For if it kinky or straight, if it black or white
Transparent or opaque
God make all a wi fi a special reason
And God don't make mistake

So if you want to criticize the Father work
Then you life going to be 'salt'
For the Creator love all a wi and look out fi wi
Even when wi have plenty fault

So galang, call mi black and bumpyhead if you want
But make sure say you say it loud
Because the Creator love me and me feel good
Fi be bumpyhead, black and proud.

(Joan Andrea Hutchinson © 1996. Reprinted with poet's permission.)

Standard English	*Patois/Dialect*
Cornrows	**Canerow**

What do you think cornrows resemble? If you guessed cornfields, then you are correct! Cornrows resemble cornfields. Hence, its name, due to the visual similarity. These tight braids laid along the scalp represented, order, agriculture and a civilized way of living. The braided hairdo was a style that could be worn every day or for more formal functions. They also wore box braids which connect to Mbalantu women in Namibia. Women in Namibia are known as "The Braided Rapunzels". Their hair is floor length. Every status change and stage of their life is reflected in their hair.

Slaves during the colonial era wore cornrows to pay respect to their homeland Africa and also because of its practicality as they labored in the sun. The treatment of enslaved slaves was dependent on the texture of their hair. If the texture and kink looked more European, better treatment was administered.

Many white tourists when they visit Jamaica get their hair braided and add colourful beads. Is this cultural appropriation or appreciation? Kim Kardashian, back in 2018, sported braids and stated they were "Bo Derek braids". Bo Derek is a white American model and actress. Again, is this cultural appropriation or appreciation?

In Jamaica, and other Caribbean countries, it is referred to as "canerows" because of slaves planting sugar cane as they wore this style. Cornrows were used in the following ways:

- A specific number of braids could mean: a time to meet up to plot a rebellion or devise an escape route.
- Seeds were hidden in cornrows, so when slaves escaped, they could plant their own crops.
- Seeds were also hidden in cornrows to provide nourishment while on the run from plantations to freedom.
- During the journey to The New World, slaves' heads were shaved. As a result, to maintain their identity, they wore cornrows to keep and remember their heritage. This act was to demonstrate rebellion and resistance to The New World Order and rules.
- Cornrows were worn on The Middle Passage so as to maintain a more "kempt" appearance.
- Enslaved African slaves used this hairstyle to "transfer and create maps to leave plantations and the home of their captors." (AfroBiz, 2019).
- Benkos Bioho, a King from Africa who was captured by the Portuguese, used women's cornrows to create maps and deliver messages. Bioho while enslaved in Colombia, created his own language using this hairstyle. He escaped slavery using this "method" and assisted many other slaves to do the same.

In the time of slavery in Colombia, the hairstyle called "departes" worn by women meant: "I need help to escape." The women wore "thick, tight braids braided closely to the scalp and was tied into buns on the top." (AfroBiz, 2019).

Retrieved from: https://www.afrobizworld.com/the-secret-meaning-of-the-african-cornrows

What is the root word in “departes?” What does that root word mean? How ingenious were our ancestors?

____

____

____

____

1. Identify two (2) rhetorical questions from text and explain its intention/ purpose based on the context in which it is used.

2. Explain the pun on the words "roots" as used in second paragraph.

3. How do you interpret "India Arie" lyrics?

"I am not my hair. I am not this skin. I am the soul that lives within."

4. What are dreadlocks?

5. Define and state the origin of Bantu knots.

6. What do wigs symbolize in the Egyptian culture?

7. Why do you think slaves with "European-looking" hair texture were treated differently?

8. Do you believe that the Japanese men are demonstrating cultural appropriation or appreciation?

9. Was Kim Kardashian demonstrating cultural appropriation or appreciation? What are your views?

10. Rewrite Joan Andrea Hutchinson's poem in Standard Jamaican English (SJE). Read both versions to your classmates. Use your notebook.

RECOGNIZING PROBLEM AND SOLUTION - GROOMING AFRO-TEXTURED HAIR

Problem: This is an issue/situation that requires a plan of action, as what is currently being faced is harmful, unwelcomed or frustrating.

Solution: This is the course of action that is taken to resolve the problem.

Answer the following before reading the passage. You may write your responses in your notebook.

Grooming Questions

GIRLS

1. How do you feel about hair?
2. Do you struggle to comb your hair?
3. What is your signature hairdo?
4. Do you like the texture of your hair?
5. How often do you wash it?
6. How often do you moisturize it?
7. Do you wear protective hairstyles?
8. Do you wish you had "good" hair?
9. How often do you wash your hair?

BOYS

1. How many times per week do you wash your hair?
2. Do you moisturize it?

3. Do you like the texture of your hair?

4. How often do you visit the barber?

5. Do you moisturize your scalp?

Grooming Afro-Textured or Kinky Hair

Taking care of one's natural hair can be a time-consuming process. For girls, wash days can be long and tiresome. Once it is wet, it can become tangled and knotted and difficult to comb or brush through. Boys have it easier as they can simply wash, apply hair products of choice and for some boys, absolutely nothing is applied to the hair after washing. They just comb or brush and go. Let us be honest here, sometimes the boys abandon even the very act of combing the hair attached to their scalp. However, Afro-textured hair when groomed properly is stunning and turns heads, but it requires care like every other hair texture.

Due to the Afro-texture, both boys and girls, have to keep their hair moisturized as our hair texture is more prone to breakage. If it is dry, then it is harder to comb through and easier to break. For girls, before attempting to comb your hair ensure it is moist. It is as simple as getting a spray bottle, filling it with water and then adding an oil of your choice. You can add castor oil, almond oil, coconut oil or olive oil and add three to five drops of rosemary or peppermint oil, shake then spritz each section before detangling. Boys do you want your hair to grow or your scalp to be in a better condition? If you do, then try the method just mentioned as well. Similarly, if you have dreadlocks this will work for you too.

Girls, when wearing protective hairstyles, still hydrate your hair and just as you hydrate your tresses, hydrate your body. Drink water! It helps with hair growth while flushing toxins from the body. On wash days, do a pre-shampoo (pre-poo). Coat your hair with conditioner then wash with shampoo. After shampooing, reapply conditioner. While the conditioner is still in the hair, attempt detangling. Do use combs that have wide teeth. Wooden combs are better as they cause less hair breakage. However, if you cannot afford a wooden comb, use a large comb with a firm wide tooth. Always oil the tips of your hair strands. Minimize wearing your afro out too often and applying excess heat. Use heat protectant when using the hair dryer or curling iron.

Both boys and girls should avoid using too much gel and edge control as they contain alcohol that dries the hair out. Dry hair equals hair breakage. Do eat greens for hair health and invest in a satin scarf or bonnet for covering head and a satin pillowcase to sleep on. Boys trim frequently. Girls trim your hair ends every six to eight weeks to get rid of split and straggly ends. Braid hair before retiring for bed and avoid tight hairstyles. Black hair is not 'nappy,' 'ugly' or 'wooly.' Do you know who in The Bible is described as having hair like wool? Jesus. When John got a vision of Jesus he described "his head and his hairs as white like wool," (Revelation 1:14-KJV). Our hair is that of our Saviour, Jesus Christ, The Messiah.

Our hair texture is not problematic, if we understand how to groom it with care and love.

I Affirm My Identity-

Read me **Aloud** with strong conviction and a winner's attitude and mindset!

My hair and skin tone make me regal, royal!

I am a leader, not a follower.

I am a warrior for Jesus Christ

I am an influencer for positive change

I am innovative. I make witty, useful and lucrative inventions.

I accept correction

I aim to stand out, POSITIVELY, and not to fit in

I am an overcomer

I am determined, highly motivated and disciplined

I honour my parents and live a life of honesty and integrity

I put God first

I am a world changer

I will excel

I am eloquent and articulate

I strive to be excellent

I am responsible

I am gifted, talented, unique, special, beautiful on the outside and the inside

I use my gifts and talents to glorify God.

I make a positive impact

I will be more successful than my counterparts

I have excellent work ethics.

I take initiative

I am bold and wise

I make a difference and make valuable contributions to society

I find solutions for problems.

I see the glass always as half full and never half empty.

I am sought after and sought out for my ideas and wisdom

I am favoured. I am surrounded only by the friends that God chooses.

I make wise decisions

I am an excellent listener, patient and possess a calm disposition

I am unafraid to walk away from situations that compromise and challenge my Christian values and upbringing.

I am a peacemaker.

I separate from instigators, haters and violent people

I am humble

I respect my body because it is the temple of the One, True and Living God.

I pray for others.

I am a child who belongs to the One, True and Living God.

1. Highlight at least three (3) problems and solutions discussed in passage about Afro textured hair.

2. Based on the information provided in text what can be done to help kinky hair grow?

3. Why should your Afro textured hair not considered problematic?

4. Explain the pre-poo technique.

5. What is the benefit of covering hair with a satin scarf or bonnet.

6. Which hair tip is too costly to even attempt?

7. Which is the most cost-effective tip seen in passage?

8. Which hair tip will you try and why?

9. How did reading the affirmations make you feel?

10. How will you apply the affirmations to your daily life?

DISTINGUISHING FACT FROM OPINION - THE BEGINNING OF RACIAL SEGREGATION AND INEQUALITY

Fact: This is a statement that is true. It can be proven. There is evidence to support or confirm its validity.

Opinion: This is a statement that is a belief. It cannot be proven to be false or true. It is based on a feeling, an attitude, or a judgement derived at.

The Beginning of Racial Segregation and Inequality

White captains arrived in Africa offering manufactured goods, weapons and rum for slaves. African kings and merchants did not hesitate because the individuals whom they chose to exchange for such commodities were criminals, debtors or prisoners of war from rival tribes. By selling their people as slaves, African kings became richer. This was bartering, but was a human equivalent to rum or a firearm? Was the exchange proportionately equal or skewed due to greed?

African kingdoms prospered from the slave trade. As the demand for slaves increased, Africans saw the capturing of slaves as an excuse to go to war. In order for tribes to protect themselves, they would sell their own people as slaves in exchange for European firearms. Sadly, those who were sold were mostly men.

The Europeans who were "Christians" justified their right to enslave Africans for two (2) reasons:

1. Africans were believed biologically inferior.

2. They believed that Africans were destined to be slaves.

They made these statements as they had purported that Christians could not be enslaved. This was highly contradictory as they had shared their faith with these slaves and if Africans were now Christians, should they be slaves?

Nevertheless, this thinking made it impossible for Africans and their future descendants, even after the abolishment of slavery, to acquire equal status and rights as their white counterparts.

1. How was inequality first demonstrated in the passage?

2. Identify one factual statement from the passage.

3. State one opinion from the passage. Why is it considered an opinion?

4. What would be the implications for Africa if the majority of the slaves sold were men?

5. Based on the passage, why did free slaves struggle for racial equality?

6. Should criminals have been sold as slaves? What are your views?

____

____

____

____

7. Since criminals became slaves, identify the character traits they would possess and how they would behave on the plantations?

____

____

____

____

____

____

____

8. How is the information that you read useful to you?

____

____

____

____

____

9. Look at the map of the world. Find the continent of Africa, then answer the following questions:

   (1) Which ocean is to the West of Africa?

____

   (2) Which two (2) bodies of water are to the east of Africa?

____

3. What is the name of the second-largest ocean and where is it situated?

____

____

____

LITERARY GENRES - HOW "THEY" TURNED US AGAINST EACH OTHER

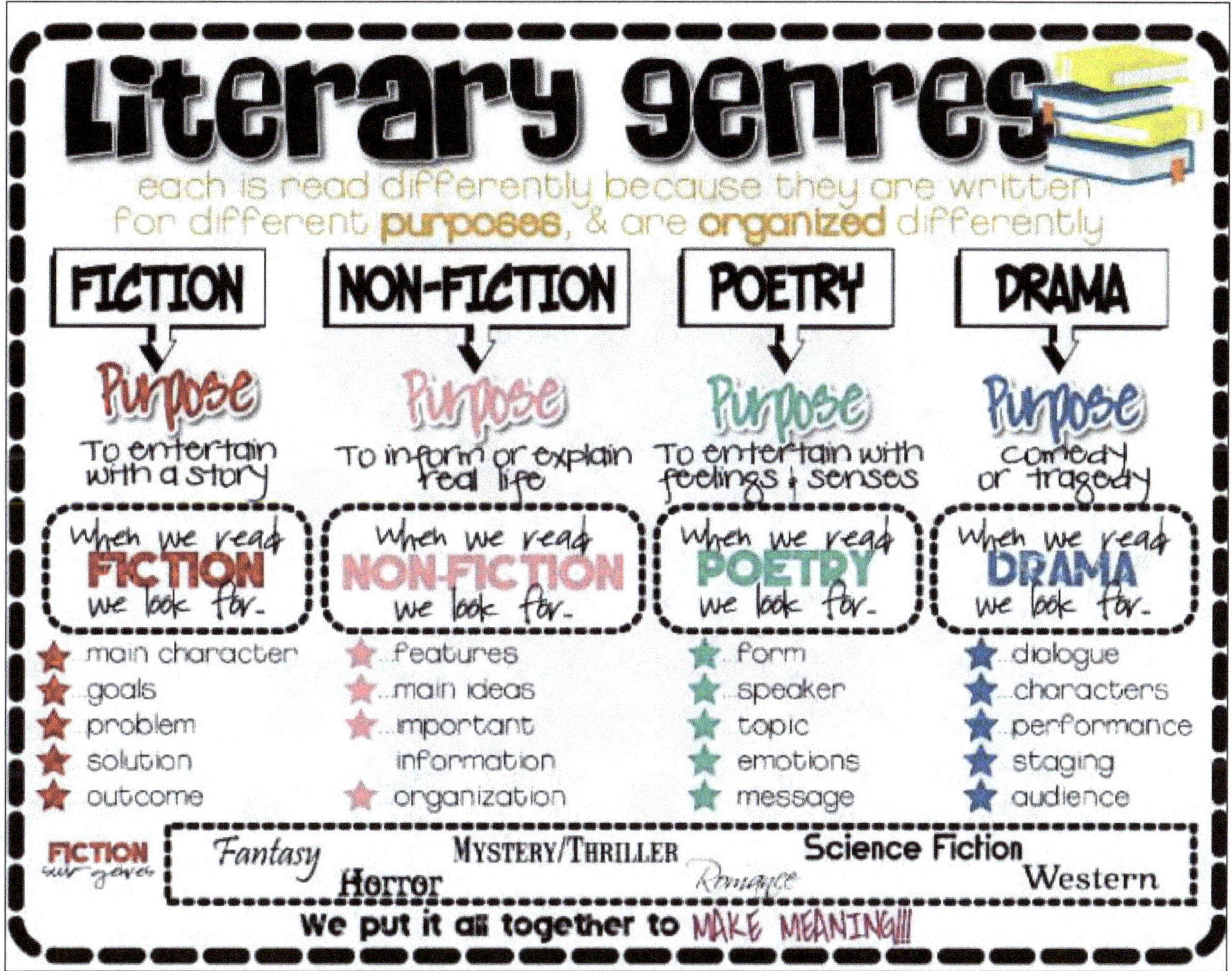

Retrieved from https://www.weareteachers.com/literary-genres/

How "They" turned us against each other.

There are many acts and injustices that occurred to the black race during slavery. Within the curriculum, history books that have been published in the past have omitted certain information either out of ignorance or an attempt to hide the truth. Here are some facts that shed light on how "they" turned us against each other.

1. The tribe leaders who were men were sodomized before their people. The goal was to emasculate them, dehumanize and belittle their manhood in the eyes of their people. This broke the will of these strong, proud men and caused their spirits to wither so that they would not have the strength to rebel or fight back.

2. The men had to watch their wives been raped. This made the wives lose respect for their husbands and no longer saw their husbands as their protectors.

3. In order not to purchase slaves, the strongest fertile man was used to impregnate all the fertile women on the plantation.

4. Families that were taken into slavery together were separated as they were sent to plantations across the four corners of the Earth.

5. They used black men and women bodies to conduct medical research without anesthesia or their consent. They perfected the practice of PAP SMEAR tests and Mammograms because of enslaved females.

6. They would blindfold the male slave, so he would not know that he was impregnating his mother.

7. They freed us without giving us land, money or any kind of recompense after their nations were built because our backs broke from over two hundred years of hard labour. We made the world rich. This fulfilled what was written in Deuteronomy 28:43-44-:

8. "The stranger who lives among you will rise higher and higher, and you will go down lower and lower. The stranger will be the head and you will be the tail." (AMP)

9. After the slaves made them rich, some had to buy their freedom. What a cruel irony as we funded the entire Western economic system for free and in bondage.

10. They sold the slaves' children to other plantation owners.

11. They brainwashed some men and women to believe that slavery was better than freedom as they were created to be enslaved. As a result, if an escape or rebellion was planned, those who believed they were no better than slaves told their slave owners about their fellow brothers' and sisters' "rebellion" or

"escape plans."

12. They degraded us and made our hearts hate our colour. Black kings and queens now fought each other for food. Brave men had now become cowards. Husbands could no longer protect their wives and children. Having children was perceived as a curse rather than a blessing as they would be taken away, used, abused and grow up in bondage.

Our ancestors were perceived as not being fully humans by slave owners, but we forgive past actions because we will create a better future. Will we not? Today, after what our forefathers went through, endured and overcame we take it all for granted. We treat each other as "they" treated us. We hate each other as "they" hated us. We fight and kill each other as "they" fought and murdered us. Our forefathers' eyes grew dim looking for a freedom that never came in their lifetime. Our freedom came at a high cost. It was blood, sweat and tears. Instead of sowing seeds of compassion, diligence, kindness, selflessness, respect and empathy, we plant seeds of discord and hate.

Why do we hate each other? Why are we not our brothers' and sisters' keepers? Why do we not work together and build our nations, this world? Imagine what we could accomplish if we worked together.

Our ancestors were separated, torn apart by force. Are we going to let "them" continue to win and see us divided? As "they" continue to kill us, are we going to assist them through our greed, envy and jealousy? We must unite in love. We must be obedient to God.

In the words of Marcus Mosiah Garvey: "UP you mighty race!"

Awake from your slumber black warriors. We are not each other's enemies.

1. What literary genre is the above passage and why?

____

____

____

2. To whom does the term "they" refer to?

____

3. What does the expression, “UP you mighty race” mean? Who is the mighty race?

4. How did the slaves contribute to medical advancement? Define the terms.

5. The slaves did not consent to their bodies being used for medical experiments. Do you believe that the black community should have been recompensed in some way?

6. State why the best properties, land spaces and businesses are not owned by blacks.

7. How can you change the narrative for future generations?

8. What emotions did reading the above text arouse?

9. What healthy, non-destructive steps or methods will you take to release or let go of the negative emotions?

Kemet people of Ancient Egypt, image courtesy of The African History

Retrieved from https://www.thecollector.com/were-ancient-egyptians-black/

VISUALIZATION - THE POWER OF THE BLACK DNA

This is using the mind to create a mental picture of what was read. Visualizing is stirred when the reader can through words, imagine the looks, touch, taste, sound and smell of an image.

Visualizing is accomplished through the use of the literary device, imagery. It evokes images and emotions that appeal to the five senses.

The Power of the Black DNA

Henrietta Lacks is the black woman who is known to possess immortal cells. Henrietta had cancer. While hospitalized, a sample of her cells were sent to the tissue laboratory. During this observation, it was discovered that her cells did not die after a few days which is typically the case. Instead they were replicating, reproducing, imitating, doubling and increasing. This was a huge medical breakthrough as the possibility to conduct research on cells outside of the body were now possible. (Black History in Two Minutes or so, 2021)

Her cells have contributed to Polio Vaccines, Chemotherapy, HIV/AIDS. Cloning and IVF (in vitro fertilization). These have all benefitted from the HeLa cell line. It is called HeLa in honour of the first two letters in her first and last name respectively. Modern medical research advancement can be traced back to a black woman who died in 1951 from cervical cancer at age thirty-one.

As the power of the black DNA is further expounded upon, it must be clear that everyone has melanin. This is factual. Melanin is a result of special skin cells called melanocytes. This protects the body from the damaging effects of the ultraviolet light. More melanin means a decreased susceptibility to sunburn and less cancer of the skin. Nevertheless, a black person can still get sunburn and is encouraged to wear sunscreen. Due to the higher levels of melanin, skin cancer for black people is lower than that of whites.

Africa is where life began. Scientists believe this. From the Garden of Eden flowed four rivers. Although the exact location of The Garden of Eden is unknown here is a scripture to analyze:

“And the name of the second river is Gihon. The same is it that compasseth the whole land of Ethiopia.” (Genesis 2:13, KJV)

Where is Ethiopia located? Did you know that Ancient Egyptians were black Africans? This means that movies that are created and aired on Netflix and other movie networks are an inaccurate depiction or representation of what the characters from Egypt really looked like in the past. Have you looked at ancient hieroglyphics? These pictographs and drawings told a story about black people before colonization.

In the book of Genesis 2:7, it reads:

“Then the Lord God formed the man of dust from the ground and breathed into his nostrils the breath of life, and the man became a living soul.” (KJV)

What colour is dust from the ground? One thing it is not, is white. Man became a living soul. The soul is the will, mind, emotions and intellect of a person. Ham is one of Noah’s son. The name Ham in Hebrew means “dark” or “black” The prophet Jeremiah asked in Jeremiah 13:23:

Can the Ethiopian change his skin, or the leopard his spots? (KJV)

Jeremiah was warning the disobedient Hebrews of Judah that they needed Yahweh to change from their evil ways. Just as an Ethiopian cannot change the black colour of their skin or a leopard its spots, they cannot change their idolatrous ways without God. Jeremiah prophesied that the tribe of Judah would be destroyed. After Solomon's death, the ten northern tribes refused to submit to his son, Rehoboam. As a result, two kingdoms of Hebrews arose. Thus, Israel to the north, and Judah, to the south. See why today there is war over which country is Jerusalem's capital? Israel was conquered by the Assyrians. They were genetically, culturally and linguistically no different from The Babylonians. Assyria is an offspring of Babylonia. Judah, on the other hand, was conquered by The Chaldeans (Babylonians). Chaldea was an ancient land in southern Babylonia. The Assyrians did not settle The Israelites in one place. They scattered them all over the Middle East and some escaped, fled. They lost their Yahweh religion and their Hebrew names and identities. There are consequences for not worshipping the one true and living God, Yahweh. (Jewish Virtual Library, 2023)

So, despite us looking so different we all share a common ancestor, Adam. Adam the man that God created from the dust of the ground. The Adam DNA that is believed to be in every man today. Geneticists through technological breakthrough and advancement can trace DNA all the way to our ancestors. DNA is the carrier of genetic information. It points us to our ancestral origins. Our genes, our heredity is that which is transferred from parent to child. The Y Chromosome DNA informs the identity of the father of the child. The Y chromosome remains unchanged in men from Africa to Jamaica and the world. For the females, mitochondrial DNA is passed on from mother to child. Both boys and girls receive this, but only the females pass it on to their own children. This mitochondrial DNA in females everywhere is similar to women from Africa.

These were the startling findings that Frank Bender a Forensic Scientist and Sculptor on National Geographic shared, and he presented a face to the world of what Adam may have looked like. The face however was not what started a frenzy of conversations and debates, but rather the skin tone. The white sculptor sculpted, molded, carved out, fashioned a black Adam. (The Boxing Historian, 2015)

There is even more compelling evidence where historians share that ancient Egyptians once called the land of Egypt and the entire African continent Kemet, meaning, "land of the black people."

Thus, the debate continues is it black or white or just the human race? What are your views?

1. What part of the text could you visualize and why? Which of the five senses did it appeal to? Comment on its effectiveness.

2. What makes The Black DNA so powerful?

3. Using context clues from the passage, give a word similar in meaning to the following:

- Sculpted
- Hieroglyphics
- Melanin
- Soul
- DNA
- Compasseth
- Representation
- Ancient
- Inaccurate
- Susceptibility

4. Why do you believe Frank Bender's findings are not discussed more via the media?

5. Has the information read, prompted you to research your black history? Outline what you would like to know more about.

6. Write a paragraph that reflects the new information that you have learned. In groups of two (2), engage in dialogue with your classmate about your discoveries.

7. In your own words, explain how Henrietta contributed to medical advancement.

SELF-QUESTIONING - WHY JESUS COULD NEVER BE WHITE

Self- Questioning: This is asking yourself questions before, during and after reading a text. This is an excellent comprehension strategy to use to gain both a deeper meaning and understanding of a story/passage/text.

- While reading you may ask yourself the following questions:
- What is the author trying to convey/say here?
- What can be inferred from this statement or question?
- What is the purpose of this genre of writing?

Before beginning write the meaning for each type of question:

Literal	***Inferential***	***Evaluative***

Now look at these questions and make the necessary jottings or notes to answer the questions.

BEFORE READING	**DURING READING**	**AFTER READING**
What do I know about this topic? (Look at the title of passage to answer this)	***What am I learning? (As you read, highlight a point or two that is new to you)***	***What more do I want to know? (Answer this after reading the passage)***

Why Jesus could NEVER be white

Jesus Christ is not white. His ethnicity and race is undoubtedly not Caucasian. This is not a racist statement. This is a fact. Jesus being portrayed as a European looking guy with white skin and blue eyes with thick, long blond hair was made popular by Warner Sallman, who painted the "Head of Christ" in 1940. He was a commercial artist and the Protestant and Catholic publishing companies used his painting on prayer cards, stained church glass, calendars, hymnals and faux oil paintings (Christ-Centered Mall, 2016). Nevertheless, scripture, scholars and the geographical location of Jesus' birth provide compelling evidence that he was in fact not white.

Let us analyze scripture, specifically some verses of Matthew chapter 1:

> 1Now when Jesus was born in Bethlehem of Judaea in the days of Herod the king, behold, there came wise men from the east to Jerusalem,
>
> 2 Saying, where is he that is born King of the Jews? for we have seen his star in the east and are come to worship him.
>
> 3 When Herod the king had heard these things, he was troubled, and all Jerusalem with him.
>
> 13 And when they were departed, behold, the angel of the Lord appeareth to Joseph in a dream, saying, Arise, and take the young child and his mother, and flee into Egypt, and be thou there until I bring thee word: for Herod will seek the young child to destroy him.
>
> 19 But when Herod was dead, behold, an angel of the Lord appeareth in a dream to Joseph in Egypt,
>
> 20 Saying, Arise, and take the young child and his mother, and go into the land of Israel: for they are dead which sought the young child's life.
>
> 21 And he arose, and took the young child and his mother, and came into the land of Israel.
>
> 22 But when he heard that Archelaus did reign in Judaea in the room of his father Herod, he was afraid to go thither: notwithstanding, being warned of God in a dream, he turned aside into the parts of Galilee:

23 And he came and dwelt in a city called Nazareth: that it might be fulfilled which was spoken by the prophets, He shall be called a Nazarene. (KJV)

From the verses, it is clear that Joseph, Mary and Jesus blended in with the black Egyptians (see verse nineteen for reference). They were unnoticeable, practically invisible. Additionally, when the white Roman soldiers came to arrest Jesus, Judas had to point out who Jesus was by planting the infamous "betrayal kiss". If he were white, with light- coloured hair and blue eyes, would Judas have to do this? This means that Jesus assimilated with his dark- skinned counterparts. He looked like everyone else.

Another scripture for point of reference is Revelation 1:14-15 and it reads:

14 The hairs of his head were white, like white wool, like snow. His eyes were like a flame of fire, 15 his feet were like burnished bronze, refined in a furnace, and his voice was like the roar of many waters. (ESV)

Burnished bronze has a medium-brown tone. Something that is refined in a

furnace or fire is smooth and dark. The scripture stated his hair was white, only the hairs on his head. What is amazing is that some will say, do not interpret this scripture literally and to this I respond:

Jesus shows up in a vision with a dark skin tone, why not white? Did he show up as himself since he is not the son of a man, so he never lies? Soul food for mental deliberation.

Keri. L. Day, who has a PH. D in Constructive Theology and African American Religion and is an Associate Professor at Princeton explains:

In the early Christian communities, there was actually an avoidance of putting images of Jesus. In general, images of God were seen as idolatry. Jesus was a Jewish man. There were all these diverse diasporas. Many of them were Afro-aesthetic and that in many ways helps us to reflect on Jesus in our contemporary language as a "person of colour." (The Root, 2018)

Co-author, Tabitha L. Jones of the book titled, "White Jesus", speaks to the proliferation of a white Jesus feeding the racial apartheid that still exists in America even today. A "white Jesus" feeds the maintenance of the white supremacy agenda. She asserts that the white Saviour mythology is an ideology that serves the interest of maintaining white power and the gospel of Jesus has nothing to do with that. (The Root, 2018)

Even if we argue that Jesus is not black, he is still not white. Jesus was born in Bethlehem, fled to Egypt and grew up in Nazareth, a village in Galilee. Galilee is in Northern Israel. Nazareth is in the Middle East and so is Bethlehem. If you look at Middle Eastern men today, and it is highly improbable that they looked like this back in Jesus' era, but for the purpose of emphasizing a point, they are still not white men. Egypt is in North Africa and again when Jesus fled there, he did not stick out like a sore thumb, he blended in and pictographs and drawings depict the Egyptians at that time as black or dark skinned. An image of a white Jesus gave plantation owners the "air" of superiority and African slaves the blunt force of inferiority.

In Deuteronomy 28:1, God states if his people, the Israelites, follow His commandments and have no other gods before him, then he would bless them but if they did not, they would be cursed. Read the following verses from Deuteronomy 28:

> 32-34 Your sons and daughters will be shipped off to foreigners; you'll wear your eyes out looking vainly for them, helpless to do a thing. Your crops and everything you work for will be eaten and used by foreigners; you'll spend the rest of your lives abused and knocked around. What you see will drive you crazy.
>
> 41 You shall father sons and daughters, but they shall not be yours, for they shall go into captivity.
>
> 43 The sojourner (stranger) who is among you shall rise higher and higher above you, and you shall come down lower and lower.
>
> 48 therefore you shall serve your enemies whom the Lord will send against you, in hunger and thirst, in nakedness, and lacking everything. And he will put a yoke of iron on your neck until he has destroyed you.
>
> 49 The Lord will bring a nation against you from far away, from the end of the earth, swooping down like the eagle, a nation whose language you do not understand, 50 a hard-faced nation who shall not respect the old or show mercy to the young. (The Message Bible)

Who do these verses sound like? Did you know that Rome is in Europe? Do you know the Romans converted to Christianity while in Africa? Do you know that when the Romans sailed to Africa the symbol on their flag was an eagle? Is it not ironic or a tad too coincidental that God said that "from the end of the earth, a nation far away will swoop down like an eagle? Is this more than a simile? The Romans were very much in Africa and The Middle East. Remember Pontius Pilate the Roman who refused to have anything to do with Jesus' crucifixion?

The curses that befell the Israelites sound very much like what unfolded in slavery. "Your sons and daughters will be shipped off to foreigners; you'll wear your eyes out looking vainly for them, helpless to do a thing." The white man shipped us to The Caribbean, Europe and The Americas.

Are we the Hebrews of a chosen generation, the descendants of Jacob, the son of Abraham, who was given the name Israel?

Would I be too forthright if I stated the truth?

We are Hebrew . We are God's chosen people and oh yes, Jesus is most definitely not white.

1. Identify and write the thesis statement.

____

____

____

____

2. For each point mentioned in the thesis statement write a supporting sentence or detail that expounds or develops each idea presented.

____

____

____

____

____

____

3. Using examples, highlight three (3) argumentative techniques that were used.

4. Identify two reasons for propagating the ideology that Jesus is white.

5. Why is Christianity not a white man's religion?

6. In what ways have the Caribbean culture and curriculum helped to proliferate the belief that Jesus is white?

7. Do you believe that we are the descendants of the Israelites, the Hebrews? What are your views?

8. Has reading this passage changed your perspective or views about religion in any way? If so, how?

Now you do! Using the argumentative essay above as a guide, choose one of the following questions to develop.

EITHER

a. A person must be judged based on their character and not the colour of their skin. What are your views?

OR

b. The positive achievements of black culture are not celebrated enough in the media. Discuss.

For the topic chosen, do the necessary research, and find suitable examples to expand or develop your points. Do use the APA format for citations. A resource that can assist you in understanding how to use citations correctly is The **Purdue Online Writing Lab**.

DETERMINING IMPORTANCE / SYNTHESIZING - BLACK WORSHIP

This process requires the reader to select the most essential information in the text to ascertain or gain a deeper overall understanding of what was read. Determining importance is separating the main ideas from the non-essential information such as the supporting details. This is like "weeding out" unnecessary information.

Synthesizing: When you are able to determine importance you are better able to synthesize. You become adept at drawing together important ideas and details in order to explain the central message of what was read. You will combine background knowledge with what you have just read to enhance your understanding. Unlike summarizing, where you cannot add your ideas, when synthesizing you can most definitely do so. When synthesizing, your original insights and perspectives are encouraged as they demonstrate a deeper understanding of the text.

Let's determine importance and synthesize together!

Scenario 1: If you were going on a beach trip and you were told to pack ONLY five (5) items what would they be and why?

Scenario 2: You are on a boat that is sinking. A deserted island is in sight. You can only grab three (3) items from the boat. What three items would you grab and why?

Scenario 3: You are at the movies with your friends. Your parents are at a wedding and they are not answering their phone. Some of your money got stolen or lost. You do not have enough left to buy lunch and pay your fare to go home. You have asked your friends and they are unable to assist you. Would you buy lunch and walk the five miles home or not eat and pay your fare to go home? What would be your choice and why?

Black Worship

There is the erroneous perception that the singing, clapping of hands, dancing and the playing of instruments are all modes or forms of worship taught to blacks by their slave masters. On the contrary, let us see what the Bible states.

Yahweh instructs in Psalm 100: 1-2:

Make a joyful noise unto The Lord, all ye lands.

Serve the Lord with gladness. Come before his presence with singing. (KJV)

The scriptures instruct us to make "joyful noise" and "sing"

In 2 Samuel 6:14 it reads:

And David danced before The Lord with all his might. (KJV)

King David a man after God's own heart "danced" before Yahweh. It may be at the forefront of your mind to ponder: was King David black? Scholars debate over this, but studies show that ancient Israel had no white people. What is therefore your conclusion? History was rewritten by those who conquered us. Our history continues to be attempted to be erased. In the 21st century The Holy Bible is subtly being changed to reflect and incorporate New Age thinking and philosophies. For this reason, the online Bible may read differently from The Bible you have at home or is owned by your grandparents or older relatives in your family. Ancient Hebrews were black until the Europeans arrived. In some bibles, the scripture may omit the name of Jesus in its translation. Is this deliberate? Why is Jesus hated so much? Why are some first world countries so intolerant of Christians, but so accepting of other doctrines?

Christians cannot worship freely in China and to speak out against certain societal issues that the Bible considers immoral is met with derision and contempt in not just first world countries. In China, the bible has been rewritten to reflect or state that Jesus participated in stoning the woman who committed adultery, instead of forgiving her. This is blasphemy! Currently, the Chinese Communist Party (CCP) has prohibited online worship. In order to share any religious content online, "Christians and churches will need an, 'Internet Religious Information License.' The catch is that such licenses will only be granted to 'legally established'-or government-controlled churches." (Landrum, 2022). You need to ask yourself this question: Why?

Psalm 47:1 instructs: *"O clap your hands, all ye people; shout unto God with a voice of triumph."* (KJV)

Remember, the Holy Bible is divinely inspired by God. It is impossible to erase the Creator of the universe from our daily lives. He is in every facet of this system. The educational system says, "obey authority." This in fact scriptural. Every authority that exists today has been instituted by God (Romans 13:1). However, you ought to obey God over man.

The law enforcement declares: "do not kill." This is actually one of the commandments in Exodus 20:13. Your teachers and parents say, "do not steal". God said it first in Exodus 20:15. You go to church and the pastor admonishes you and preaches, "obey your parents." Again, God stated it first in Exodus 20:12.

However, any Bible that states that you are gods is wrong. We are sons and daughters of the Most High God. For those who read Psalm 82:6 and believe that the scripture is declaring human beings are gods must reread for understanding in "context." We, human beings are ALL mere mortals. Lucifer (Satan) is not a god. Fallen angels are not gods. Demons are not gods, but anything you idolize can become a god: money, friendships, sex, scamming, jewellery, fashion trends, the latest gadget, pornography, your figure, your complexion, your hair. If you love it more than God, then you worship it. Exodus 20: 3 reads:

Thou shalt have no other gods before me.

This includes yourself. Instead pray to God. This is a form of worship. Daniel worshipped God three times a day through prayer. Praying keeps your heart centered on God and not worldly possessions. When you pray, pray for the peace of Jerusalem that God will show mercy and favour at His set time. As you pray for the peace of Jerusalem, you are also praying for the peace of Jamaica because God has arranged things so that no other place on Earth can achieve permanent peace until there is peace in Jerusalem. Pray that God sends a revival to Jamaica and heal our land.

Worship God because he is a part of EVERYTHING. When you say the name Yahweh, its syllables are the inhalation and exhalation of air. He is our breath of life. No matter how much they attempt to erase our history and change the Bible, they can never remove Yahweh. He is and will always be, the supreme authority. Worship Him.

1. What would be the central conflict in the passage just read? Would it be, *man vs. society, man vs. man, man vs. self or man vs. nature*? Why?

___

___

___

___

2. Using the template below, determine the importance of details in passage.

Determining Importance Template

Name:			Date:
Text title:			
Sentence or paragraph number	'Who' or 'what' is the sentence or paragraph about?	Most important thing about the 'who' or 'what'	Interesting but not important

Retrieved from https://www.ricpublications.com.au/blog/post/encourage-determining-importance-as-a-strategy-in-the-classroom/

1. Write a summary of passage. Do not exceed 80 words.

2. How should you worship Yahweh?

3. What should you not worship and why?

4. As a teenager, what are some of the things that you currently focus on? Identify at least three (3). Why?

Before proceeding, close your eyes and **quietly pray** for the peace of Jerusalem and Jamaica. Pray for a revival to begin in our land. Ask God to bless and heal our land. Ask God to bring swift justice to those who delight in committing acts of crime and violence.

POST SLAVERY...

Retrieved from https://face2faceafrica.com/article/story-of-the-suit-that-represented-decolonization

BIAS AND PERSPECTIVE - THE DRESS CODE THAT EMBRACED DECOLONIZATION

Bias- The use of language that shows the reader that the source is strongly for or against the person or event being described or spoken about. The language is intentional and may be considered unfair. With bias there is favouritism, partiality and prejudice.

Perspective: This is the viewpoint from which an individual may perceive or see an event, person or thing. For example, two individuals may watch the same movie but they both saw different things. Neither is right or wrong, their viewpoint, outlook, position or vantage point just differs from each other. Perspective is simply the way you see something.

The Dress Code that Embraced Decolonization

From jacket and tie to Kareeba! This was an attire created by renowned Jamaican fashion designer Ivy Ralph. She is the mother of actress, Sheryl Lee Ralph. Her Kareeba (Kariba) suit left the shores of Jamaica and was worn in Ghana, Tanzania, Barbados and Guyana.

After independence from Great Britain, Jamaican men thought that the jacket and tie was both stifling and inappropriate for Jamaica's tropical conditions. Such attire was believed to represent the colonization of the "planter." It reflected domination and mental oppression. To break from such a fashion stronghold the "stylish open-neck, over- the- pants Kareeba and matching trousers suit evolved into the country's official standard for formal occasions, work attire and everyday wear." (Calys-Tagoe,2022).

In other countries it was referred to as the safari suit. The PNP administration in 1972, under the leadership of the Right Honorable Michael Manley embraced the Kareeba suit. It became the official uniform for the Peoples National Party (PNP) which was symbolic of them breaking from the past and embracing independence. The Kareeba jacket had the look of a bush jacket, but the matching jacket and pants gave the total look its name. Ivy Ralph's Kareeba had no epaulets and the usual two patch breast pockets.

When the Jamaica Labour Party (JLP) came into power, it was declared that the Kareeba suit was inappropriate for politicians. The parliament then declared, "MPs, guests and media should dress with decorum." (Calys-Tagoe,2022).

Ivy Ralph in 1999 received the Order of Distinction for her extraordinary work in advancing fashion. The Kareeba suit became the "it" name regardless of the manufacturer.

Today, the Kariba suit is not known as it was in the past. Fashion has evolved, and designers have added their own spin, cut and fashion. However, it is still worn by men who embrace its artistic and visually appealing look.

1. Reread the passage and identify two (2) statements that reflect bias.

____

____

____

2. Identify two (2) statements that reflect perspective.

____

____

____

____

3. Can you think of any current fashion fad that lends itself to bias or perspective?

____

____

____

____

____

____

4. Label each statement as true of false.

i. The Kareeba suit is a bush jacket. _______

ii. The Kareeba suit was created in the 1970s. _______

iii. The Kariba suit is still worn today. _______

iv. The Right Honorable Michael Manley made the suit popular. _________

v. Jamaica was the only country that wore this suit. _______

vi. The Kariba suit was stylish to everyone. _______

vii. Ivy Ralph received an award for the suit she created in Africa. ________

viii. The suit is still the same today. ____________

ix. JLP administration contributed to the loss in popularity of the Kariba suit. ____________

x. Decolonization is embracing black culture. ____________

FLASHBACK

A flashback is an interruption in the chronological order of the story. It is used to add suspense, interest, drama and intrigue. It reflects an occurrence of events that unfolded before the actual story begins.

For example, a movie may begin with a present-day scene, then the words, "a few days earlier" flash across the screen. The movie's plot then begins and shows all the events that occurred that led to the scene that started the movie.

Elements of a Short Story

The eight (8) elements of a short story are:

1. Setting- This is where the story takes place. This entails date, day, time, year, place and social period.
2. Characters- The people, animals and things whom all the action revolves and who engage in dialogue directly or indirectly.
3. Plot- The beginning, the middle and the end of the story.
4. Conflict- This is the problem or challenge that arises.
5. Resolution- The manner in which the problems or challenges are resolved.
6. Theme/s- The central idea, message, moral or lesson of the story.
7. Point of View- The viewpoint from which the story is told. This can be first, second or third person.
8. Style- The manner in which the writer uses sentences, sentence structure, literary devices or techniques to convey the story. It is simply the use of words to express thoughts or ideas that is uniquely the writer's way of writing.

Madame C.J. Walker

If you choose, you may colour or shade each line drawing

MADAME C.J. WALKER, FROM POVERTY TO AFFLUENCE

Meet the first black self-made millionairess who became famous for her hair products. She invented the hot comb and the world's first hair-straightening formula, "Madame Walker's All- Purpose Conditioning Crème". Upon her death, in 1919, her network was estimated to be one million (1,000,000) US dollars which today would be the equivalent of at least six million (6,000,000) US dollars. Her beginnings, however, had not been one of wealth, influence and glamour. In fact, it had been quite the opposite.

Madame C.J. Walker had been born Sarah Breedlove on December 23, 1867. Her life had been eventful. Her parents died when she was only seven. She was married at fourteen and became a single mother to a young daughter at twenty, after the death of her husband. An unremarkable life thus far that appeared to be destined for failure as she had been born on the plantation where her parents were once slaves. As a widow, to make ends meet she was a washerwoman who earned a dollar fifty per day. She was on the verge of being homeless. The stress took its toll and so Sarah began to experience hair loss in her early thirties.

To salvage her hair, she began using a product made by another black woman called Annie Turbo. From here, Sarah made the transition from not only using the product but also selling it. Sarah married again and changed her name to Madame C.J. Walker. Her entrepreneurial skills grew, and she decided to start her own hair line. She reported that her hair ingredients manifested itself in a dream. She went on to start her company. She sold, "Madame C.J. Walker's Wonderful Hair Grower." As her company expanded, so too did the range of hair products that she sold.

She became a door-to-door salesperson and recruited other black women and shared her entrepreneurship skills. She paved the way for women of colour to own businesses. Currently, in The US there are approximately 5.4 million women entrepreneurs. This is what black girls must emulate: ambition and hard work, regardless of economic status or background.

Upon her death the headline read:

Mrs. C.J. Walker, Real Estate Operator Made Fortune in Few Years.

Mrs. C. J. Walker, known as New York's wealthiest negress, having accomplished a fortune from the sale of so-called anti-kink hair tonic and from real estate investments in the last fourteen years died yesterday morning at her country estate at Irvington-on-Hudson.

Retrieved from: https://youtu.be/mfB1VRE7s7E?si=FipN9AXXj502Kt5d

1. How was flashback used in this passage? Comment on its effectiveness.

2. Highlight three (3) struggles that Madame C.J. Walker faced and overcame.

3. Why do you think she changed her name?

4. What is the moral of this story?

5. Why do you believe women were on a quest to get the "kink" out of their hair?

6. What prompted Walker to create her own hair care line?

7. What work ethics from the millionairess can you apply to your own entrepreneurship journey?

8. State the elements of the short story.

9. Using information from the passage create an advertisement for one of Walker's hair products. Be creative.

CAUSE AND EFFECT - BLACK WALL STREET

Cause: WHY the events happened/occurred.

Effect: The RESULT of the events that unfold/happen/occur.

Some Cause and Effect Transitional terms:

- Since,
- Thus,
- Hence,
- Consequently,
- Therefore,
- Accordingly,
- As a result

BLACK WALL STREET

In 1921, Greenwood in Tulsa, Oklahoma, was one of the wealthiest black communities. It was thus the hubbub for African- American businesses, and it was known as The Negro Black Wall Street.

It was populated by wealthy African-Americans who ran successful businesses. In Greenwood, there were schools, a library, a hospital, hotels, theatres and so much more. It was a thriving town that was filled with black people. Under Jim Crow's Law blacks were forbidden to shop at white owned businesses. "Jim Crow" was a contemptuous slang term that was intended to belittle and insult the black man. It came to mean any state law passed in the South that reinforced different rules for blacks and whites. Hence, these laws were passed to maintain and uphold white supremacy.

Since, Black Wall Street existed during a time when racial tension was so thick the air was pervaded with its HATE. As a result, the tangible manifestations of this hate were the thousands of lynchings that took place. Lynching was murder carried out by a white mob with the compliance of the law enforcement. Consequently, the Greenwood Massacre, an inhumane atrocity, against blacks unfolded with the white law enforcement doing absolutely nothing and even participating in murdering innocent black people.

Greenwood, the epitome of black progress was burnt to the ground and three hundred people died. More than twenty black churches, a hospital, a funeral home, a school, a theatre, doctors and lawyers' offices, hotels, grocery stores, restaurants and hundreds of homes utterly destroyed by fire. Over a thousand buildings burnt and the possessions of black people were stolen and placed in the homes and businesses of white people. Three hundred people were murdered, simply because of the colour of their skin and over forty city blocks burnt down!

The Black Wall Street Massacre lasted for two days, on May 31, and June 1, 1921. The historical successes of a black race had been erased, eradicated and consumed in the flames of racial contempt.

1. In your own words, summarize the Greenwood massacre.

____

____

____

____

2. What did Black Wall Street symbolize?

____

____

____

3. What is white supremacy?

____

____

____

1. Identify the cause and effect relationship for the destruction of Black Wall Street?

5. Do you see evidence of another cause and effect relationship in the passage? Write and explain it.

6. What does the term "inhumane atrocity" mean?

7. If you had lived in Greenwood in 1921, based on the passage what were some activities that you could not do?

8. How would these restrictions have impacted your thoughts/feelings/emotions?

9. Is racism still present in the 21st century?

10. Using the format for an e-mail, do write an e-mail to a friend outlining what Black Wall Street was, what happened, the causes and effects of its destruction. Do use cause and effect terms to begin sentences.

MAKING INFERENCES - STRANGE FRUIT HANGING FROM A TREE

This is to make reasonable assumptions based on information provided in a story. Inferring means drawing conclusions based on the evidence read in the text. In this context, the text is song that was once a poem.

Background Information: The following is a song recorded in 1939. The song is an outcry against the injustices suffered by blacks at the hands of whites, specifically a cry against lynching. When the song was recorded, lynching was still unfolding. Black people were hung on a tree and left to rot. The white police officers were onlookers as blacks were lynched. The pictures of their bodies were taken and posted in the newspaper or on postcards and sent around the country. You may listen to the song before reading its lyrics.

STRANGE FRUIT HANGING FROM A TREE

Strange Fruit. Sung By Billie Holiday. Written and Composed by Lewis Allan (1939)

Lyrics

Southern trees bear strange fruit
Blood on the leaves and blood at the root
Black bodies swinging in the southern breeze
Strange fruit hanging from the poplar trees

Pastor scene of the gallant south
The bulging eyes and the twisted mouths
Scent of magnolias, sweet and fresh
Then the sudden smell of burning flesh

Here is a fruit for the crows to pluck
For the rain to gather, for the wind to suck
For the sun to rut, for the trees to drop
Here is a strange and bitter crop

Retrieved from: https://www.austincc.edu/dlauderb/1302/Lyrics/

StrangeFruitLyrics1937.htm

1. Based on the context, what kind of fruit did southern trees bear?

2. Why is the fruit considered strange?

3. After the blacks were lynched, what is another act that was done to them? Quote the line and stanza that supports this.

4. Explain in your own words what is happening in stanza/verse 3.

5. With evidence from the song, outline the senses that its lyrics engage?

6. What is the tone of the song?

7. What mood(s) do the song evoke?

8. Identify the theme/s seen in song.

9. Now that you have read the poem, draw the image/s that its lyrics painted in your mind's eye

“Separate from them. Let’s build our own schools.”

—— Malcome X

TONE : MALCOKM X

This is the author's voice, feelings, opinions that become evident throughout the text. This may become evident through the characters, the narrator or the author's emotions, attitudes or views.

Malcolm X demanded black dignity and black respect "by any means necessary".

When Malcolm was incarcerated, he joined the Nation of Islam. It was a religious movement led by Elijah Muhammad. Malcolm X was of the belief that slavery terminologies such as "coloured" and "negro" should become obsolete and be replaced with more dignified references such as "Afro- Americans" and "black". Malcolm X's ideologies were the foundation and birth of Black Power activists.

After President Kennedy was assassinated, Malcolm X remarked:

"Chickens coming home to roost never did make me sad; they've always made me glad!"

This resulted in a rift between himself and the Islamic leader. He was assassinated by Islamic gunmen as four hundred people in a ballroom watched.

Nevertheless, his philosophies have inspired movements such as: "Fight the Power". His belief was that black people should take control of their own destiny.

Martin Luther King Jr's words thus resonated in the end when he stated that Malcolm X's violent methods to obtain black equality would "reap nothing but grief".

1. What is the tone of the passage?

____

____

2. What religion did Malcolm X practice?

____

____

3. "Chickens coming home to roost never did make me sad; they've always made me glad!" Explain the meaning of this statement.

4. Malcolm X advocated for black dignity by "any means necessary" What do you believe this means?

5. What caused the rift between Elijah Muhammad and Malcolm X?

1. Who is an activist?

"We must all learn to live together like brothers."

—— Martin Luther King Jr.

MOOD : DR. MARTIN LUTHER KING JR.

This is the emotion/s that the writing evokes or arouses within you after reading. Essentially, it how YOU feel after reading the text.

Dr. Martin Luther King, Jr

Martin Luther King, Jr was born on January 15, 1929 in Atlanta, Georgia, He studied theology at Crozer Theological Seminary and received his PhD from Boston University in 1955. His family roots were in the Baptist Church.

His protests or demonstrations for unity between blacks and whites were done peacefully. In his famous speech, "I Have A Dream" he declared:

"I have a dream my little children will one day live in a nation where they will not be judged by the colour of their skin but by the content of their character."

In his speech as a guest at Barrat Junior High in South Philadelphia Dr. King orated:

"Be a bush if you can't be a tree. If you can't be a highway just be a trail. If you can't be the sun, then be a star. It's not by the size that you win or fail. Be the best of whatever you are."

A few months after giving this speech, he was assassinated. Reverend King was assassinated whilst trying to educate the offsprings of former slaves about their civil rights.

Although Martin Luther King, Jr advocated for blacks to protest for their civil rights peacefully, his death sparked riots across the country. His adoption of nonviolent resistance to achieve equal rights for Black Americans earned him the Nobel Peace Prize in 1964, four years before his death.

1. Highlight the pervading mood/s in the text.

2. What kind of speaker was Dr. King? Support your responses with examples from text.

1. Why do you believe he was killed?

1. Based on the information that is presented in the passage, create a poem about Martin Luther King, Jr.

COMPARE AND CONTRAST

Compare means to highlight or state the similarities.

Contrast means to point out the differences.

Transitions of Comparison: similarly, in the same way, in similar fashion, at the same time, by the same token, likewise, both, also, compared to.

Transitions of Contrast: otherwise, in contrast, nevertheless, on the other hand, regardless, in spite of, notwithstanding, conversely, on the contrary, alternatively, whereas.

You have read about Malcolm X and Martin Luther King, Jr. Let us do a compare and contrast composition.

Before you compose your ideas, use the Venn Diagrams OR T-Chart below to highlight the similarities and differences.

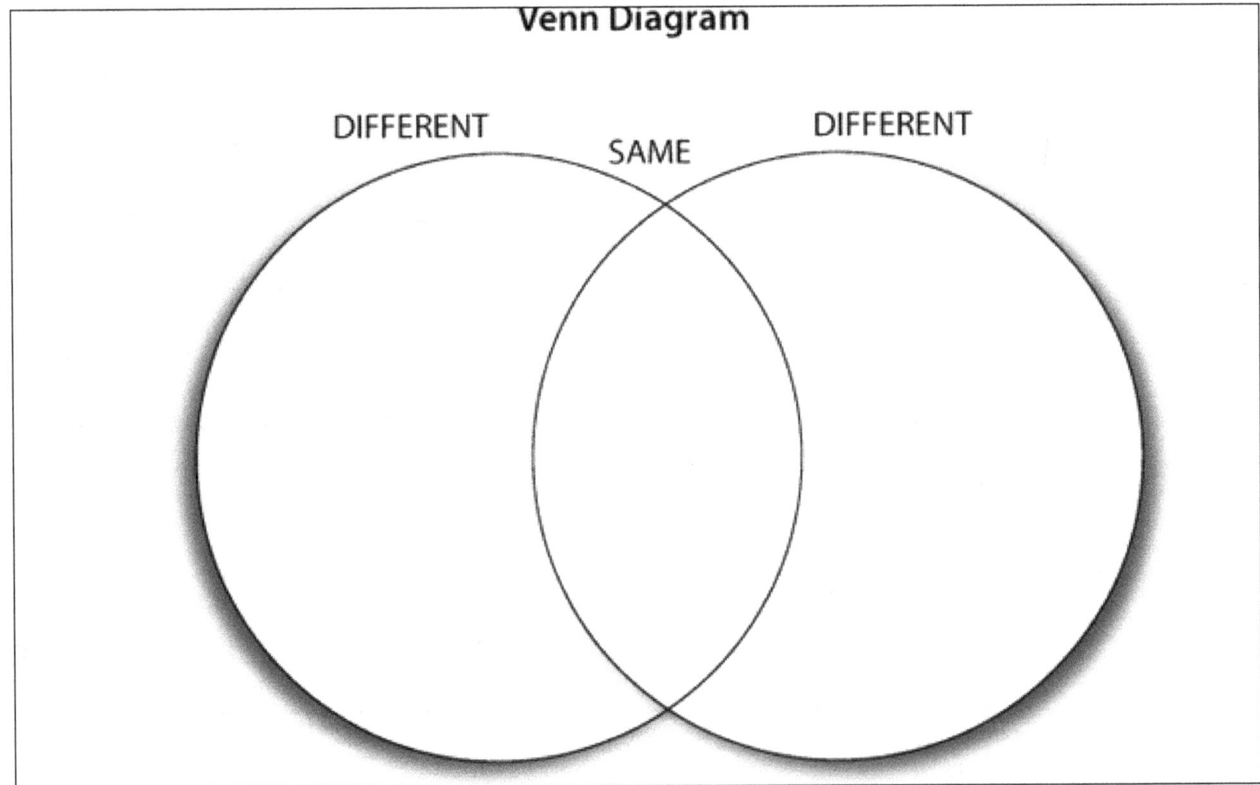

If you need additional space for writing, draw your own Venn Diagram or the T-Chart.

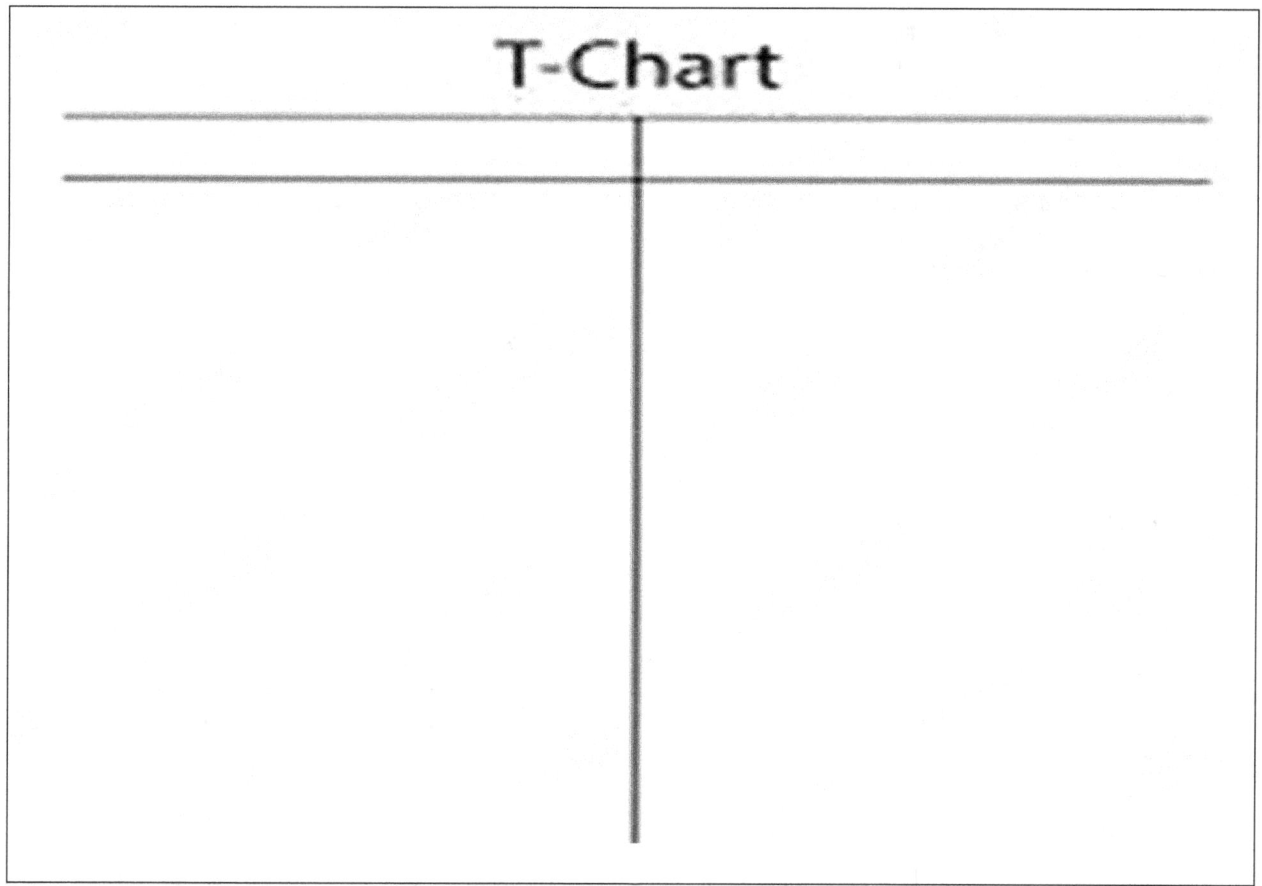

Observe the details stated in Venn Diagram or T- Chart and now incorporate all such details in composition. Do use the appropriate transitions for comparing and contrasting.

Format for Compare and Contrast Essay

Step 1: Write a title for essay.

Step 2: Introduction

- Sentence 1: Start with a fact about civil rights or a rhetorical question.

- Sentence 2: Write one fact about Martin Luther King Jr. that relates to civil rights.
- Sentence 3: Write a factual statement about Malcom X that relates to civil rights.
- Sentence 4: Write a thesis statement that indicates/states that you will be comparing and contrasting Martin Luther King Jr. and Malcolm X.

Step 3: Paragraph 2

- Discuss similarities between Martin Luther King Jr. and Malcom X.

You may begin like so:

Malcolm X and Martin Luther King, Jr were both civil rights activists. Similarly, they were orators who were powerfully influential.

Step 4: Paragraph 3:

- Highlight the differences between the two (2). Do use contrast transitions.

Step 5: Paragraph 4:

- Share why it is useful or important to know the differences between Martin Luther King Jr. and Malcolm X. You may add a new, related sentence to the topic.

____

____

____

____

____

____

____

____

Marcus Garvey

SEQUENCING EVENTS : MARCUS GARVEY

This is simply writing information in the order it appeared in the passage/poem/text/movie/video. Transitional or sequential terms like first, second and third are used to outline the order of events.

Marcus Mosiah Garvey- Leader, Advocate, Jamaican National Hero

Marcus Mosiah Garvey founded the Universal Negro Improvement Association (UNIA) in 1914. It was his goal to unite all blacks across the globe. In 1916, Marcus Garvey, a Jamaican on a powerful mission migrated to The United States. **Marcus Garvey, the Jamaican National Hero that contributed to American Black History.**

His goal was to encourage every black person to return to Africa to improve their industrial, commercial, educational, social and political conditions. Garvey migrated to The US during a tumultuous period as blacks were frequently being lynched in The South. As an orator whose words could stir action, he spoke with conviction to blacks in America, making it clear that their place was never going to be in The United States or Europe - it would be in Africa.

To bring his repatriation into action, he creates "The Black Star Line". This was a steam ship line built to transport blacks back to Africa. The purpose was to have African Americans invest in these line or fleet of ships that would transport thousands back to a colony that would be established by Garvey, but a colony controlled by negroes.

His passionate advocacy got the attention of The American Government, specifically, J. Edgar Hoover of the Federal Bureau of Investigation (FBI). The first set of Negro agents were hired to carry out this investigation. He was convicted of mail fraud with The Black Star Line. He was tried, convicted and placed in jail in 1925. He was deported to Jamaica in 1927. Garvey was banned from ever reentering The US. He later died in London, after a stroke, in 1940.

His "Back to Africa" movement cannot be undermined as he created the largest black political movement ever in the history of America. He was a beacon of light to both the Anti-Colonial Movement and Black Nationalist Leaders.

Marcus Garvey, the father of the Modern Back to Africa Movement.

1. Outline the order of events in Marcus's life right up to his death.

2. Who is an advocate?

3. How did Garvey demonstrate this advocacy?

4. Do you believe Garvey was guilty of mail fraud? Write your views.

5. What does anti-colonial mean?

6. Had the negroes successfully returned to Africa, do you believe they would have prospered?

7. Why did Garvey's Back to Africa Movement fail?

8. What steps or strategies do you believe he could have taken to ensure this undertaking would have been a success? Outline steps/strategies in a sequential order.

THE AUTHOR'S PURPOSE - BLACK INVENTORS

This is defined as the reason or intention for writing. An author may write to:

- Instruct/teach/inform to provide factual information
- Entertain: to amuse, humour
- Persuade: to convince, to agree or see a perspective/viewpoint
- Explain: to clarify, explain or simplify a complex topic/concept
- Argue: to provide relevant ideas/opinions/facts to present a sensible case for an idea/position/stance

Black Inventors

Many people have heard of Thomas Edison, the inventor of the incandescent electric lamp and the motion picture projector. Few, however, have heard of Lewis Latimer, the black inventor who perfected and improved Thomas Edison's original light bulb.

Latimer had a brilliant mind and taught himself Mechanical Drawing while working in a patent office. Latimer ingeniously figured out how to make the carbon filament in the light bulb last longer and therefore be more useful.

Latimer sold one of his patents in 1882 to The United States Electric Lighting Company. This led to a strong friendship developing between him and Thomas Edison. A white and black inventor working side by side in a laboratory; he played a pivotal role in the burgeoning of the Electric Lighting Business. (Black History in Two Minutes or so, 2021).

A Black Female Inventor

A woman as an inventor? It may sound incredulous, but it is very true. Her name is Sarah Boone and in the late nineteenth century, she created something that you still use today.

Historically, people would iron by placing a wooden plank between two firm surfaces. Sarah Boone was a black skilled dressmaker. She was determined to make the process of ironing clothes easier and more effective. As a result, she thought that a simple rectangular ironing board would prove to be more useful to iron clothes, especially women clothing. Hence, she thought if the board was both rectangular and curved at one end this would be perfect! Boone was granted a patent in 1892 for her invention.

She was the fourth African American woman to be awarded a patent in the history of The United States. However, do you see how her invention has transformed a simple task like ironing across the globe?

When you look at the light bulb and the ironing board, remember black inventors had a role in something you use today.

Will you be the next black inventor?

1. What is the author's purpose for this genre of writing?

____

____

____

____

____

____

2. Provide three (3) examples from text to prove the author's purpose.

____

____

____

____

____

____

____

____

3. What is a patent?

4. Explain what Lewis Latimer invented.

5. What current invention do you think you could perfect or improve?

6. Please do explain how you would go about making such an invention better or greater?

Is there a problem that is currently affecting your country or globally?

Create a machine, a structure, a robot, a building, or an idea that can solve the problem.

Follow these steps:

Step 1: What problem do you want to solve in your country or globally?

Step 2: How do you plan to go about solving it? Think it through.

Step 3: What will you need to create your invention? Who will be invested in your completed creation or benefit the most?

Step 4: Where will you go to meet your ideal clients? Outline the steps you will take to make people know about your invention?

Think, invent, and then implement.

Share with your school, your community and your nation.

Be sure you can explain HOW your creation will provide a solution. You are a problem-solver.

Get to WORK!

If you want to, here is a space, to draw a SKETCH of your INVENTION.

Nelson Mandela

IDENTIFYING THEMES : NELSON MANDELA

A theme is the message or idea that resonates throughout an entire text. It is expressed not as a word, but rather as a sentence that conveys a moral, a lesson, a truth that is applicable to real life. Throughout a work of literature, the themes may come to light through the story telling process and it its elements- setting, character, plot, conflict, resolution, style (use of language) and tone.

Nelson Mandela- The Transformation from Political Prisoner to Global Hero

Nelson Mandela became the first black president of South Africa on May 10, 1994. He was a lawyer, politician, social rights activist and philanthropist. Mandela was passionate about equality for blacks. He lived during a time when the white minority ruled, oppressed, and encouraged segregation by promoting black inequality and hence inferiority to whites.

Mandela's protests were done in a non-violent manner, but he was disliked by white law enforcement who viewed him as a threat to the peace of the nation and the continued compliance of blacks to work in subservience and submission.

In 1956, he was charged for treason. Treason is the conspiracy to overthrow the government. This is known as a political crime. The Treason Trial was from 1956-1961. He, and all others involved were acquitted. In 1962, he was rearrested as he continued his fight against the anti-colonial, systems and government. They charged him for inciting workers to strike and leaving the country to go to England without a permit. He was sentenced to life imprisonment. He spent twenty-seven years behind bars for believing and actively promoting that blacks should have equal rights as whites. Mandela's time behind bars had the global nation in an uproar that started the anti-apartheid protest and the cry to, "Free Mandela"

Mandela fought against the apartheid that existed in South Africa even while in prison. The segregation between blacks and whites left the blacks in a state of oppression and Mandela represented black resistance against the stifling injustice that permeated their existence. He fought for equal rights and his influence increased behind bars rather than diminished.

In 1999, when Nelson retired, he established the Nelson Mandela Foundation.

This organization works to promote the principles of equality, freedom and peace. To this day in South Africa, July 18, which is Mandela's birthday, is celebrated as "Mandela Day" in South Africa,

Nelson Mandela the symbol of the anti-apartheid struggle coined the phrase, "It always seems impossible until it is done."

1. Identify two (2) themes that are evident throughout the text.

___

___

___

2. Support each chosen theme by providing relevant examples and explanations from passage.

___

___

___

3. Define the term, "apartheid"

___

___

4. What is meant by the "anti-colonial systems?"

___

___

5. Write five (5) facts about Nelson Mandela.

___

___

___

___

6. What does Mandela symbolize? Explain this symbolism.

Mandela stood up for what he believed in. Is there something that you believe in, that you will stand up for? Do you have a cause or a passion for an issue, organization, belief system? Is there something you want to bring awareness to or change?

Create a poster, flyer or newsletter to bring awareness to your issue of concern. Then, print as many as you can and share at church, school, and/or business places.

A change must come when you peacefully push!!!

FIGURATIVE LANGUAGE - THE WAY

This is when the writer deliberately chooses NOT to use literal language to convey a meaning. Such a choice adds deeper meaning to the text and makes the effect more powerful or impactful. Figurative language is figures of speech. Some figures of speech are:

Analogy: A comparison between two things, people, events to show the similarities or the relationships.

Symbolism: The use of symbols to represent ideas or qualities. It is a concrete image to represent an abstract idea. It is representational imagery.

Irony: Verbal irony occurs when the speaker or narrator relays something that may be humorous, but there is an obvious difference between what is said and what is truly intended or meant. What is stated is the opposite of what is truly meant.

Metaphor: This is comparing two things without using "as" or "like". It is simply stating that something is.

The WAY

There has been much debate that Christianity is a white man's religion, as they had misused the scriptures to assume dominance or control over the black slaves they had captured and sold in The Caribbean, The US and Europe. For the blacks to believe this misguided concept and remain submissive, the majority were never taught to read or write. They were illiterate adults who raised illiterate children. However, this was a lie. Christ did not condone slavery and as soon as free slaves could read and write, they saw that "the way, the truth and the life" was a path of freedom from oppression through Christ Jesus and overcoming mentally what they had endured for approximately four hundred years.

Before the Europeans arrived, Moses is sent to speak to Pharaoh to let the Israelites go who had been in bondage in Egypt for almost four hundred years. Ironic is it not? History repeating itself? The Israelites worshipped the one true and living God, "YHWH" (Yahweh). The Israelites had migrated to Egypt because of a famine, but their status as guests soon became that of slaves. They were strong and kept having children. They soon outnumbered the Egyptians who feared that their increasing numbers may someday lead to them overpowering and enslaving them. This was the belief of the new Pharaoh who decided to make them slaves. A preemptive act on his part, warranted and produced out of fear rather than facts. The Israelites cried out to YHWH and he sent Moses to intercede on their behalf. Christ had not yet been crucified but Moses was introduced to make "the way" for the true Saviour. The analogy is evident.

Fast forward, Christ is crucified. Saul (Paul) is a Roman soldier who kills Christians for believing that Jesus has resurrected. Africa became inhabited by Romans through conquest (war) and colonization very much like Jamaica that was under the British monarchy or rule until 1962. Saul hates Christians. He would persecute them or capture and bind and bring them back to Jerusalem. He, however, had an encounter with Jesus and was saved. He literally saw a light shine from heaven and was blind for three days. When his sight returned, he got baptized into the faith or what was called "The Way". Saul who became known as Paul, was converted and believed in the resurrection of Jesus Christ. Paul then began to preach the Gospel (Acts 9)

Then, there is The Ethiopian eunuch who is introduced to Christ by Phillip. A eunuch is a male that has been castrated or due to a birth defect is incapable of reproducing or one who chooses to abstain from sexual activities so as to remain pure to God and do his work without distractions. This eunuch was of great authority, He served under Candace, Queen of The Ethiopians. He was in charge of all her treasure (Acts 8:27).

The Kushites/Ethiopians were a black group that was feared in Africa. The name Kush means "dark-skinned". They were known for their prowess in warfare. The Ethiopians were known as "the lion of war". Moses, the Israelite, married an Ethiopian.

Joseph was sold into slavery by his jealous brothers. He was brought to Egypt. While there he found favour in his master's eyes and he was appointed head of his estate. However, his master's wife wanted to have sexual intercourse with him, but he refused. She lied that he had tried to rape her and Potiphar, her husband, consequently threw Joseph in prison. While in prison he still served God and was released, when only he could interpret a dream that Pharaoh (the ruler) had. Joseph, however, through Jesus Christ made "the way" for his brothers who had to travel to Egypt for food when a famine had begun (Genesis 37). What was meant for harm worked out for good.

YHWH, the one true and living God was making his way across Africa.

Let the stigma die, The Christian's way is no white man's religion. The proof is in the Holy Bible.

1. Identify the use of irony observed in text and explain its effectiveness.

2. Why is there an analogous relationship between Moses and Jesus Christ?

3. What does "the way" symbolize?

4. (A) Who is referred to as 'the lion of war?'

4. (B) Explain the figurative language used in question 4a? Which sense does it appeal to?

5. Write five things you have learnt from reading this passage:

Ask your teacher's permission, and take turns sharing with your classmates.

DRAW A PICTURE OF BOB MARLEY

PARAPHRASING - BOB MARLEY

This is similar to summarizing, but you must show your comprehension of the text, video, movie, passage, poem by stating it in your own words. The ideas presented must be restated, rephrased or rewritten using your own language. Paraphrasing goes beyond using a thesaurus to simply substitute synonyms for the author's words. The sentence structure must also be reworded so as to clearly differentiate between the author's words and yours without changing the original meaning or ideas conveyed in text.

Question: What is your favourite novel, song or movie? Turn to your classmate and tell him or her about it. Guess what? You just paraphrased!!!

Bob Marley- A Cultural Icon

Bob Marley was born on February 6, 1945 in Nine Mile, St. Ann. His mother, Cedella was a descendant of slaves and his father Captain Norval Sinclair Marley was a privileged white politician working for The British government. Though Robert Marley was born in St. Ann, he moved to Kingston, Trench Town.

Bob Marley's parents got married, but as soon as Cedella got pregnant, Norval abandoned his responsibilities. Cedella was eighteen when she got married and Bob' s father was forty-one years her senior. He died when Bob was ten years old.

In 1976 while in Trench Town, an assassination attempt was made on his life. By then he had gained popularity and was seen as a symbol for Jamaica. He refused to take political sides and opened his home to troubled youths.

The year 1976 marked fourteen years since Jamaica had gained its independence from The British and commodities were scarce, tension was high and political hatred had erupted. Political parties begged for his endorsement as his words carried weight, but Marley chose to stay neutral.

On December 3, 1976 an assassination attempt was made on the life of Bob Marley. He, his wife Rita, and his manager – Don Taylor, we shot. All three survived. He left for London and he released his album, "Exodus" in 1977 while residing there. That same year he injured his toe while playing soccer (football) and noticed a small dark spot under the nail.

It was the first sign of melanoma- the cancer of the skin.

Marley refused traditional cancerous treatments due to his Rastafarian beliefs. The practice of Rastafarianism is a hybrid religion that incorporates Christianity, mysticism and Black Nationalism. The message of this movement was black pride, freedom for oppression and hope of returning to Africa one day.

This cultural icon's body was viewed by twelve thousand Jamaicans and another ten thousand waited outside. Decades later his music has only increased in popularity. His songs were filled with peace, love, compassion, unity, black power and positivity. Which Bob Marley song is your favourite?

The Rise of Reggae Music

Singer, songwriter and musician Bob Marley blended Reggae, Ska and Rocksteady and became a musical legend.

He formed the band The Wailers in 1963 and they recorded "Simmer Down", a song that was written by him. It was a phenomenal success! In 1974, the band separated, and Marley started his solo career. It led to global recognition.

Marley has been credited with spreading both Jamaican music and the Rastafarian Movement. Many of Marley's songs made biblical references namely:

- Give Thanks and Praise
- Exodus
- Small Axe
- Africa Unite

Some other well-known hits are:

- Get Up Stand Up
- No Woman No Cry
- Redemption Song
- Trench Town Rock

Marley is inducted in The Rock and Roll Hall of Fame in 1994. He died on May 11, 1981.

1. Paraphrase the passage just read.

2. How old was Marley when he died?

3. What factors do you believe contributed to Marley's musical success?

4. Do the research and look at the lyrics of one of Bob Marley's songs. Answer the following questions based on its lyrical content:

   a. What pervading theme is evident in the song?

b. What literary devices were observed that added deeper meaning to the song.?

c. How can you relate to the song? How do you connect to it mentally or emotionally? Explain.

Claudine Gay

SUMMARIZING : CLAUDINE GAY

This is writing the main ideas of a passage in your own words. It must be concise. The first sentence must contain the text's title, author's name and main point of text.

Step 1: Find the topic sentence for each paragraph. Write each down.

Step 2: Find a supporting detail for each topic sentence. Write below topic sentence.

Step 3: Using your own words, write a summary that incorporates the topic sentences and supporting details. Always adhere to the word limit.

Do include in your summary, action verbs to begin each sentence in your summary writing: For example: The author **notes**, He **acknowledges**, She **adds**, The article **highlights**...

Do avoid the following:

- Quotes
- Statistics
- Abbreviations
- Opinions
- Regurgitating word for word what was read or stated

Claudine Gay- Harvard University's First Black President

Harvard University was found in 1640. It is an Ivy League School in The US that determines admission of the highest standards. It is a favourite choice for celebrities, the elite and affluent. However, on September 29, 2023 something momentous unfolded, the thirtieth president inaugurated for this school was black.

Claudine Gay who is the immigrant of Haitian parents has made history as the the first black woman to lead Harvard University. She is also the second woman in this role since the university's almost four hundred years of existence. She was formerly the Dean in The Faculty of Arts and Sciences and earned her PH. D. in government from Harvard in 1998.

Gay was elected after an intensive search. She is described as a "person of bedrock integrity." (Bacow, 2023). Claudine Gay who is a wife and a mother stated:

> *"The courage of this University-our resolve, against all odds-to question the world as it is and imagine and make a better one, it is what Harvard was created to do."*
>
> *Representation is necessary so others too can believe that as a black person, "If she can, you can, then I can too."*

Yes, to black leadership and being a trailblazer for breaking stereotypical barriers.

Unfortunately, Claudine Gay is currently being investigated for plagiarism observed in her dissertation and being "chastised" for an anti-Semitism statement made. It is thus a possibility that by the time this book is published, things may have changed somewhat. Will the outcome be negative or positive? Research and find out.

1. State the topic sentence for each paragraph.

____

____

____

____

____

____

____

2. For each topic sentence written above, write a supporting detail.

____

____

____

3. Based on the points that you have highlighted, construct a summary that does not exceed eighty (80) words.

4. What is anti-Semitism?

5. Do you aspire to hold a leadership post in the future? What qualities do you believe you ought to possess in order to lead effectively and efficiently? List at least four (4).

Colin Luther Powell

7 JAMAICANS THAT MADE THEIR MARK IN BLACK AMERICAN HISTORY

RECOGNIZING CHARACTER TRAITS : COLIN POWELL

This speaks to the feelings, emotions, qualities, thoughts, choices, morals, values, beliefs and habits of a character. Character Traits encompass an individual's personality. Their traits can be physical, emotional, mental or moral. Every individual has distinct attributes or qualities that make up their overall personality or character. Characters have multiple character traits.

Character traits may be seen directly (stated explicitly by author) or indirectly (through characters' speech, thoughts, effects on others, actions and looks)

Colin Luther Powell- April 5, 1937- October 18, 2021

Colin Powell is the son of Jamaican immigrants. He was the first African American to hold the positions of chairman of Joint Chiefs of Staff (1989-93) and Secretary of State (2001- 2005). Powell grew up in The Harlem and South Bronx sections of New York. George Bush was The President at the time that he held the position of chairman of The Joint Chiefs of Staff. This is a high-ranking U.S. military officer. His role was to give the President and other civilian leaders advice on military issues.

Powell chose not to run for US presidency, but he did speak out on national issues. He was an author, top soldier, diplomat and national security advisor. His speech at The United Nations in 2003 helped pave the way for The United States to go to war in Iraq.

Mr. Powell's qualities made him popular with Americans. He was blunt, straightforward and possessed admirable leadership qualities and skills.

Despite being vaccinated, he died because of complications caused by COVID-19. He was also battling cancer at the time of his death.

1. Citing examples from the passage, state the character traits of Colin Powell. Give three (3) examples for each.

- Direct character traits

- Indirect character traits

2. What character traits do you believe one must possess to be an excellent leader?

3. What are some positive character traits that you possess?

4. Highlight the character traits you have that you need to improve on to make you a better person.

5. How did Colin Powell contribute to Black American History?

6. How old was he when he died?

Angella Reid

IDENTIFYING THE FLASHBACK TECHNIQUE : ANGELLA REID

This is a scene that occurs before the story begins. It interrupts the flow of the story and is an indication at the beginning of the text, movie or play that this has already happened.

ANGELLA REID, LADY EXTRAORDINAIRE

Angella Reid receives the Grio Award! This is a Black Media Powerhouse that celebrates Black Excellence. Why did she receive it? The story unfolds as follows....

Angella Reid was born in St, Thomas, Jamaica. She attended high school in Kingston. She holds the prestigious position of being the first black woman appointed as Chief Usher of The United States White House.

She held the position during the period of Barack Obama's presidency. From October 2011- May 2017, she worked without complaints but was fired during Trump's administration. This course of action was both unexpected and unusual. Her job description entailed managing butlers, maids, housekeepers, chefs, curators, electricians, plumbers, engineers and cooks. She would oversee construction, renovation projects, maintenance and food service. It was also a part of her role to ensure that The President and his family were comfortable in their private quarters.

Reid is the ninth person to be named Chief Usher in the history of The White House. It was a career that started at the Half Moon Club in Jamaica and the general manager for several elite hotels, before her title in The White House.

As a result of her achievements as a black woman, she was recognized by The Grio Awards in 2012.

Explain how flashback is used in the text and comment on its effectiveness.

Why do you believe Reid was let go during Trump's administration?

Does the Chief Usher of The White House's job appear difficult? Give reasons for your response.

What may have prepared her to excel at the role of Chief Usher in The White House?

Lester Holt

COMPREHENDING CHRONOLOGICAL ORDER -: LESTER HOLT

This is arranging events in the order that it occurred one after the other.

Example:

6:00 – Said a prayer

6:15 – Got out of bed

6:30 – Had a shower

7:00 – Ate breakfast

Lester Holt- An Award-Winning Career

Lester Holt's Jamaican roots come through his grandparents on his mother's side. Holt has had an eventful career. In 1979, he worked at San Francisco Radio Station. Two years later, he started working at ***CBS*** for nineteen years as a reporter. One year later, he joined an affiliate TV Station of CBS as a reporter and an anchor. In 1986, he became the evening anchor at ***WBBM-TV***, a CBS station in Chicago. In 2000, he joined ***MSNBC.*** Three years later, Holt moved to ***NBC Nightly News*** and for the morning show Today.

In 2007, he was a full-time weekend anchor at NBC Nightly News. In 2015, he was appointed interim anchor of the weekday NBC Nightly News.

The Jamaica Observer Edition, on July 29, 2012, reported that Lester has visited Jamaica three times. During Covid-19, on February 26,2020 it is reported that a cruise ship he was on was denied access at Ocho Rios Port because a crew member displayed symptoms.

In October 2021, Lester Holt the award-winning journalist of Jamaican descent was inducted in The National Association of Broadcasters' Broadcasting Hall of Fame.

1. Arrange in chronological order Lester Holt's career.

1. Create a chronological order of your achievements or milestones.

Maurice Ashley

MAKING CONNECTIONS- TEXT- TO- SELF : MAURICE ASHLEY

This is simply linking what was read to your experience/s, your feelings and your own life.

For example: While reading a text/story/passage, you may remark:

"This reminds me of when I went to the beach. I almost drowned too."

Maurice Ashley- The Chess Player

What is your favourite sport? Do you have a passion for it? Is it something you never tire to do and time fades into oblivion whenever you begin the process of engagement? There is an individual who can so relate to these feelings.

Maurice Ashley is a chess player who was born in Jamaica, but migrated with his family to Brooklyn, New York at the age of twelve. He is the first African American to earn an International Grandmaster Chess Title. He learned chess and excelled at it. His passion and enthusiasm for chess caused him to create and do many things applicable his favourite sport. A few examples are:

- iPhone app designer
- puzzle inventor
- motivational speaker
- ESPN communicator

Consultant with universities, chess clubs, schools, celebrities and executions on how chess principles and strategies can be applied to improve business practices and assist with personal growth.

Due to his immense contribution to the game, he was inducted into The US Chess Hall of Fame in 2016 and The Brooklyn Technical High School of Fame in 2018.

1. Write/explain your favourite game/sport.

2. How can you turn your passion for your favourite game/sport into income/passion?

3. Can your passion become a business?

4. How can you leave a legacy through your passion?

5. If you had to create a logo for your business what would it be?

6. What would be your business slogan?

7. What would be your advertising strategies? List each.

Clive Campbell

FOCUSING ON TEXT-TO-WORLD : CLIVE CAMPBELL

This is a reading comprehension strategy that highlights or showcases how content in a text can be related or compared to broader issues or current news in the real world or the global society. Text-To-World connections (influences) may speak to cultural or social issues. It may relate to universal themes, global perspectives, and so help the reader to think critically and see the correlation of the relevance of the text beyond its immediate story or content.

Clive Campbell- The "Father" of Hip Hop

Herc was a disc jockey. He is credited as being the founder of Hip-Hop. This is both a genre of music that entails four elements: rapping, graffiti, painting, B-boying and deejaying. Hip hop is both a musical and cultural movement.

Deejay (DJ) Herc was born in Jamaica on April 16, 1955 in West Kingston, Jamaica and migrated to The Bronx, New York in 1967 at the age of eleven. He was nicknamed Hercules by his classmates due to his size and his love for lifting weights. His prodigy as a hip-hop legend was influenced by individuals like James Brown, and Jamaica's drum and bass.

Many people are of the opinion, that when he was sixteen and was the DJ at his sister's party in 1973, Hip Hop was born. He became known as the "Father" for influencing future DJs and their techniques.

Hip-hop music emerged from parties of The Bronx and eventually it spread from the underground onto the radio. The first hip-hop record was released in 1979 by a group referred to as Rapper's Delight.

Hip-hop became a mode of expression for inner city youths who sung about the economic and social conditions that they lived in.

"Don't push me cause I am close to the edge. I'm trying not to lose my head." Say what? It's like a jungle sometimes. It makes me wonder how I keep from going under." (The Message, Grandmaster Flash). This song reflected the struggles of this time through the lens of this rapper. This was his lyrical message.

As hip-hop grew, it influenced the fashion industry globally, so rappers wore oversized garments, bold colours, huge chains, gold teeth and Kangol bucket hats.

This genre of music was, and still is, an expression of a rapper's current reality.

Let's connect this text to the world!

1. Do rappers today still rap about present social, economic and political issues? Give an example. Write a quote that reflects the connection between their lyrics and what is currently happening in the world?

2. How has reggae music influenced fashion locally and globally?

3. In Jamaica, are there artistes from the inner city who sing about current social and economic issues and global occurrences?

4. Is Hip-Hop relevant in society today?

5. Explain the term, "Father" of Hip-Hop.

6. Outside of hip-hop and reggae, is there a genre of music you enjoy listening to? Does its lyrics reflect what is unfolding in society presently? How so?

Bessie Stringfield

TYPES OF CHARACTERS : BESSIE STRINGFIELD

A **Dynamic** character changes throughout the story. This character will learn a lesson because of the events relayed in the story surrounding him/her. The lesson results in a permanent change.

A **Flat** character does not change throughout the course of the story. These characters are simple, few details are provided, and they are usually minor characters.

Bessie Stringfield- "The Negro Motorcycle Queen"

Betsy Lenora Ellis was born on February 9, 1911 in Kingston, Jamaica. She was the offspring of a black and white union. After her birth, her parents migrated to Boston, Massachusetts where they contracted small pox and died. Betsy was only five years old when she became an orphan.

However, she was adopted by a wealthy, white, Irish, Catholic woman. It is unclear when she began being referred to as "Bessie". Her adopted mother gifted her on her sixteenth birthday with a 1928 Indian Scout motorcycle. At age nineteen, in 1930, she started travelling across The United States. As racism was prevalent then, she was often denied accommodations, so she would sleep on her motorcycle at filling stations with her jacket serving as a pillow or with black families who were gracious enough to open their doors to her.

To earn money, while on her journeys, she entered and won many flat track races, but was frequently denied the prize money due to her gender. She would pretend to be a man and enter the races but as soon as she took off her helmet, the winning cash prize would be denied.

During WWII Bessie Ellis started carrying secret documents for the army on her Harley-Davidson bike. She was the only female in her unit.

During her travelling, she married and divorced six times and had three miscarriages. In 1950, she ended her motorcycle escapades, bought a house in Miami, Florida and became a licensed practical nurse. She continued riding Harleys to church as a senior citizen. She would own a total of twenty-seven over her lifetime. As Bessie would say:

"I never bought anything used-except husbands."

Ten years after her death in 1993, The American Motorcycle (AMA) instituted the Bessie Stringfield Award to honour women who are leaders in motorcycling.

In 2002, she was inducted into The Motorcycle Hall of Fame.

1. What type of character is Bessie Stringfield? Support your choice with evidence from text.

____

____

____

____

____

____

2. What problems did Bessie face?

____

____

____

____

____

3. How did she overcome these problems?

____

____

____

____

____

4. How does Bessie differ from the stereotypical roles of women?

5. Do her character traits remind you of anyone? Do you see yourself in her mannerisms, attitudes or actions?

Sheryl Lee Ralph

FORESHADOWING : SHERYL LEE RALPH

The prefix "fore" means occurring beforehand. It is foretelling or forecasting a future event.

Foreshadowing is a hint, warning or clue of what is to occur.

It tells what is to come later in the story. The signs may be seen through the use of language, imagery and/or symbolism.

Sheryl Lee Ralph – The Jamaican American

Sheryl Lee has never been one to shy away from her Jamaican ancestry. The lineage is a result of her Jamaican mother a fashion designer Ivy Ralph who designed the Kariba suit. This suit was made popular by then Prime Minister of The PNP (People National Party), the Right Honorable Michael Manley. The Kariba suit became a style trademark for PNP politicians. It was an open neck over the pants shirt and matching trousers suit.

Ralph's father was an American college professor, so her schooling took place in Mandeville, Manchester and Long Island New York where she was born.

On January 15, 2022, Ralph made history as the second ever black woman since 1987 to win The Emmy Award for best Supporting Actress in a comedy series. The movie titled, "Abbott Elementary" which has an almost all black cast, revolves around educators in an underfunded public school in Philadelphia. She was a first-time nominee at age sixty-six and won for the first time. She remarked during her interview on TVJ (Television Jamaica) on ER (Entertainment Report) with Anthony Miller that she had worked for forty years before winning an Emmy to become an overnight sensation.

The National Association for the Advancement of Coloured People (NAACP) also gave her acknowledgement by nominating her for the same film. She did not win but the recognition of her talent and role in the film is definitely an admirable feat.

During an interview on September 11, 2023, on TVJ, Entertainment Report, she stated that she felt more Jamaican than American, hence she refers to herself as, "Jamerican". She stated her true admiration for the Jamaican educational system that educated her as currently there is a "dumbing down" of the educational content in American schools. She expressed her parents' desire for her to receive her schooling in Jamaica as it was a better fundamental start.

Ralph was vocal about the number of principals and teachers she meets in The States which is a sure indicator of the "brain drain" that is happening in the educational system.

The Jamaica Observer, on July 2, 2023, reported that Ralph was selected to receive a star on The Hollywood Walk of Fame. She was given the title of "Order of Jamaica" the nation's fifth-highest honour for her contribution to the international film industry.

On February 2023, she performed at The NFL Super Bowl finals. She sung, "Lift Every Voice and Sing" and this rendition is known as the "black national anthem".

During COVID-19, she donated fifteen tablets to Chantilly Primary School in Manchester. Sheryl Lee Ralph promotes Jamaica every chance she gets. She is a true cultural ambassador.

1. Actress Sheryl Lee Ralph spoke about the "brain drain" that is happening in the educational system due to the migration of principals and teachers. What does this foreshadow about Jamaica's educational system? Explain.

2. How do you think the issue/problem of “brain drain” can be solved in the Jamaican economy? Provide at least three (3) possible solutions.

3. Sheryl worked for forty years before winning an Emmy. What does this reveal about her character?

4. Why is Ralph considered a cultural ambassador for Jamaica?

5. What does the term, “dumbing down” mean?

6. Why do you believe the Jamaican educational system is considered by Ralph to be superior to America’s educational system? Give at least three (3) reasons.

KNOWLEDGE APPLIED IS POWER!

ANALYZING - WHAT "TRULY" MAKES YOU JAMAICAN

This is looking at the details of how an author writes. Observations are made to their choice of words, sentence structure, use of literary devices and tone to see how they have conveyed their thoughts, so you can formulate opinions or grasp a deeper understanding of what was read.

Discuss the following questions among classmates before standing to read the pledge aloud. Please listen to each other.

Do you love being a Jamaican? Give reasons for your responses.

What is one thing you wish you could change about your country?

In what ways do you contribute to the society? Are you a part of the problem or a part of the solution?

What does it mean to be a productive citizen?

How can you demonstrate integrity at school?

How can you represent your country positively?

What does it mean to be patriot?

How are you currently demonstrating patriotism?

Everyone stand and read aloud.

National Pledge

Before God and all mankind, I pledge the love and loyalty of my heart, the wisdom and courage of my mind, the strength and vigour of my body in the service of my fellow citizens; I promise to stand up for Justice, Brotherhood and Peace, to work diligently and creatively, to think generously and honestly, so that Jamaica may, under God, increase in beauty, fellowship and prosperity, and play her part in advancing the welfare of the whole human race.

What 'truly" makes you a Jamaican

A pledge is a solemn vow or promise. It is a verbal contract that is to be upheld. It is a commitment to uphold your end of the bargain by guaranteeing through spoken assurance, that to the best of your ability you will do everything you have declared. You have before witnesses sworn to be and become what you have stated.

The nation's pledge was written by Reverend Hugh Braham Sherlock. He was born in Portland, Jamaica on March 21, 1905. As you read the pledge you observe that three organs are needed to fulfil your promises. They are: your heart, your mind and your body.

Your country needs three parts to be involved and engaged in making this nation great and the ripple effect is that you will be great also. When these three organs work in unison then you will develop the character traits: justice, brotherhood and peace. Do you love your country? Do you love the people of this nation? Do you want your nation to be great? Are you proud to be Jamaican?

When you recite the pledge you make a promise to both God and mankind. That is not something to be taken lightly. You have promised God that you will use your heart, mind and body to advance this nation. Are you a liar? Are you a coward?

The freedom to vote, to choose who you want to marry, to go to school, to go to church and to simply sit and observe nature were acts your ancestors fought for.

To be a man or woman of your word is an honourable thing. It will make others respect and trust you. It will make you grow up to be responsible adults and citizens. Such behaviours and qualities are needed from individuals to make this country even greater than what it currently is. Will you play your part in advancing the welfare of the whole human race? Being responsible, kind, helpful, thoughtful, disciplined, loving and hard-working students are attributes that will always be trending. Do not let society fool you. The ones who choose the path of violence, live it up, but die young. Yes, you can die other ways, but are you going to help kill yourself?

What truly makes you a Jamaican is your commitment to building your country rather than destroying it. What is your choice? Which side do you choose?

1. Why does the pledge require your heart, mind and body to be involved to uphold and maintain this nation's success?

____

____

____

____

____

____

____

2. Name the attributes/actions that you pledge with your heart.

3. Name the attributes/actions that you pledge with your mind.

4. Name the attributes/actions that you pledge with your body.

5. What do you promise to stand up for? Use the dictionary to define each term.

6. Explain what it means to work diligently and creatively.

7. Explain what it means to think generously and honestly.

8. How can Jamaica increase in beauty, fellowship and prosperity?

9. Identify your role/s in the Jamaican economy so that the welfare of the whole human race can advance.

Althea Laing

IDENTIFYING POINT OF VIEW (POV) : ALTHEA LAING

This speaks to who is telling or narrating the story. There are three main views from which a story can be told or narrated. They are:

- 1st person- The reader knows because of the use of the pronoun, "I" in the storytelling process.
- 2nd person- The reader knows because of the use of the pronoun, "you". This narration is the least popular.
- 3rd person- The reader knows because of the use of the pronouns, "he" "she" or "it" as the story is being told.

Jamaica's First 'Supermodel' – Althea Laing

She is a Jamaican that has graced the covers of Essence Magazine in 1986 and 1992. Her lips were considered her greatest facial asset. Althea possessed the kind of "signature lips" that women today will pay substantial amount of money to dermatologists and cosmetic surgeons to have. This is achieved by injecting Botox to enhance their lips so as to achieve the aesthetic appearance of being plump and voluptuous. Althea Laing has these, naturally.

She won Miss Jamaica Fashion Model at age twenty-nine. She said on E-Live Unplugged during an interview on CVM that:

"I was just pursuing my dream. It wasn't even about the money because black models weren't paid well back then. I was paid a 100US to just be a fit model for Vogue because in those days a black girl couldn't be in Vogue, but today black girls are actually on the pages of Vogue."

Althea explained that as a fit model she was a standard size. Designers would thus have her try on different outfits, take pictures of her in it, but actually have white models showcase the outfits. She expressed that it was her dream to one day see black models in Vogue Magazine. Althea Laing was a model at a time when African-Caribbean women were not embraced because of their colour in the modelling industry.

"I am happy, I was able to blaze a trail for these dark-skinned girls to follow. Because of me, these girls can now aspire to be on the cover of a magazine." (Johnson, 2017)

From Jamaica to New York, she placed Jamaica on the international modelling scene. Despite having a modelling career at an age that is considered old for that industry, she created a platform for future black girls to see and emulate. Althea Laing, the supermodel who has achieved celebrity status and international recognition in the fashion industry.

She is a Jamaican trailblazer!

1. What point of view is the story being told from?

2. Using information from the text, define a supermodel.

3. Using details from the text, state how Althea Laing has inspired dark-skinned girls.

4. How has the fashion industry evolved?

5. Identify the theme/s that resonate throughout the text. Use examples to support theme/s.

6. Why did Althea pursue modelling?

7. Define a "fit model"

8. Highlight the character traits of Althea Laing. Use evidence from text to support each.

9. What is her most admirable quality? Why?

10. In what ways has this story inspired you?

JAMAICA
BOLT

TEXT -TO- TEXT : USAIN BOLT

This is simply connecting what you have read to another familiar text. You may assess the familiarities between characters, the plot, the setting, the problem, the culture, the point of view, style of writing and the resolution.

Read the passage below and see if you can assess how you can connect it to another text, article or book you have read.

Usain Bolt, To The World!

Usain Bolt moved from his hometown in Trelawny to train in Kingston Jamaica. This was arranged by former Prime Minister, PJ Patterson. He had enjoyed football (soccer) but his coaches at his former high school William Knibb steered him in the direction of track and field.

In 2002, at The World Junior Championships in Kingston, Usain Bolt became the youngest junior gold medalist. He was fifteen years old. At 6 feet 5 inches, Bolt does not possess the typical sprinter frame, but he broke a record that had been held for thirty-six years when he won at the Jamaican championship. He ran a 200 metres sprint and clocked in at 19.75 seconds and simultaneously broke a record while setting a new one. Three months prior, at the Olympics, he set a new world record in New York. In 2008, at the Beijing Olympics he won the 100 metres sprint. At this same event, he became the first and the only athlete to dismantle three Olympic and World records.

Dr. The Honourable Ambassador Usain Bolt OJ has set world records in both the 100 and 200 metres sprint. He is dubbed as "The Fastest Man Alive" and "World's Fastest Human." Bolt is so fast that he broke his own record. He did this in 2008 at the 12th International Association of athletics Federations (IAAF) World Championships in Berlin, Germany. He broke his previous 100 metre sprint record of 9.69 seconds and set a new time of 9.58 seconds.

The Honourable Usain Bolt is described by his mother Jennifer Bolt as a "natural" She noted that his gift to run was obvious from age twelve. Throughout Bolt's career, he has had setbacks, but it never deterred him from continuing to train. Some of his accolades include:

- "Sports Man of The Year" in 2011, 2009 and 2008 from RJR.
- "Man of The Year Award" in 2009 and 2008 by The Gleaner.
- "Champion for Sports Award" by United Nations Educational, Scientific and Cultural Organization (UNESCO), just to highlight a few.

Bolt has two siblings and when he visits Trelawny the people love his humility. He loves to visit his home and eat his favourite meal of pork and dumplings. These days Bolt is running in the restaurant and music industry and other entrepreneurial activities.

He is one athlete that has put Jamaica on the global scene in track and field.

1. Can you connect this story to another text? If not, read "Raymond's Run" by Toni Cade Bambara from A World of Prose, then make the text-to-text connections.

____

____

____

____

____

____

____

____

____

2. How has Bolt set Jamaica on the world map through track and field?

____

____

____

____

3. Write the topic sentence for each paragraph.

4. Why did Bolt relocate to Kingston?

5. Why do you believe Bolt excelled in track and field?

6. Which parish does Bolt hail from?

7. Based on the passage what are Bolt's most admirable qualities?

8. "Bolt is running in the restaurant and music industry" What literary device is used here? Comment on its effectiveness.

Circle the correct response.

9. Trelawny is in the county of:

   a. Surrey

   b. Cornwall

   c. Middlesex

10. Bolt was a "natural" runner. "Natural" in this context means:

a. gifted

b. effortless

c. innate talent

11. Kingston is the capital of:

a. St. Andrew

b. Jamaica

c. Portmore

12. "Some of his accolades include". Give a synonym for accolades as used in this context

a. Awards

b. Praises

c. Approvals

13. How old was Bolt when he became a junior gold finalist?

a. 13 years old

b. 15 years old

c. 14 years old

PREDICTING OUTCOMES : THE JAMAICAN BOBSLED TEAM

This is analyzing text to decipher in advance what will happen in the story. The reader will use hints, clues to foresee what may be the possible outcome, end, result or to simply see what will happen next.

The Jamaican Bobsled Team- From Sun to Snow.

Meet the legendary forefathers who decided to enter The Winter Olympics despite living on the tropical island of Jamaica. This team showcased and made the world recognize that Jamaicans could not only excel at track and field.

The Jamaican four-man bobsled team made their debut in Canada at the Winter Olympics in Calgary, Alberta in 1988. They did not officially finish and crashed during one of their runs. They inspired The Walt Disney Motion Picture, "Cool Runnings." Was Jamaica discouraged? Absolutely not!

They returned in 1992 to The Winter Olympics in France but finished poorly. Did they give up? No! They qualified again in 1994 in Norway. What do you think occurred this time? They came in fourteenth ahead of The United States, Russia, Australia, France and Italy. Jamaica continued to push and entered The Winter Olympics in 1998, 2000 and 2002. Something miraculous unfolded in 2000, The Jamaican Bobsled Team won the gold medal at The World Push Championships in Monaco!

In the lyrics of Jamaican singer Jimmy Cliff:

"You can get it if you really want

You can get it if you really want

You can get it if you really want

But you must try, try and try, try and try

You'll succeed at last."

(isit the Mystic Mountain in Ocho Rios to get the bobsled experience.

1. Do you think the bobsled team can win again? What is your prediction? State your reasons.

2. What theme/s resonate throughout the passage? Express the theme/s in a sentence.

3. Why was The Jamaican bobsled team considered the underdog in The Winter Olympics?

4. The movie, “Cool Runnings” is on YouTube. Watch the first twenty minutes and answer the following questions:

a. What is the setting?

____

b. Who is/are the protagonist/s?

____

c. What is the conflict?

____

d. State the theme/s observed thus far.

____

____

____

____

____

e. “Handsome as a lion.” What literary device is this? Explain its effectiveness.

____

____

____

____

____

____

____

____

Mae Jemison

TRANSITIONS : MAE JEMISON

These are sometimes referred to as linking words as they connect ideas, sentences and paragraphs. They are placed at the beginning of sentences to maintain coherence and cohesiveness of the text/passage. After a transition, there is a comma. The transitions chosen will be based on the type of essay that one is writing. However, some frequently used transitions are: Therefore, Thus, Accordingly, As a result, ***Afterwards, Additionally, Furthermore, Nevertheless, For example, On the other hand, Finally, Firstly, Secondly, Lastly, Consequently***.

Mae Jemison- The First African- American To Travel To Space

Jemison grew up watching "Apollo" airings on TV. This was a NASA (National Aeronautics and Space Administration) program that had American astronauts making a total of eleven flights to space and walking on the moon. **However**, she was upset that she saw no female astronauts. **Consequently**, she became inspired after seeing a female actress play the role of an astronaut on The Star Trek television show.

Unfortunately, Jemison experienced racism in her class as she was the only African American at Stanford University in California. **Nevertheless**, in 1977, she graduated with a Bachelor of Science Degree in Chemical Engineering and a Bachelor of Arts Degree in African- American Studies. **Furthermore**, she then went to medical school and graduated with a Doctorate in Medicine from Cornell Medical School in 1981. She then applied for the Astronaut Program at NASA. **Additionally**, in 1987, she was one of the fifteen people chosen out of two thousand applicants.

Equally important, she embarked on her space voyage on September 12, 1992. Jemison and six other astronauts went to space on the space shuttle Endeavour. **Moreover**, this made her the first African American woman in space. Jemison has been inducted into The National Women's Hall of Fame. Therefore, my question is this:

What will you be the first to do?

The future is waiting for you to make history. History is waiting for your legendary footprints. Make your mark. Leave a trail, called LEGACY.

1. Make a list of all the transitions in the passage.

2. Write two (2) paragraphs about your best friend. Please include the transitions written above in the story. Your story may be either descriptive or narrative.

3. How important is it to you to see people of your colour and gender in the media? How does it make you feel?

4. How did Mae Jemison leave a legacy?

Dr. Gladys West

LISTENING COMPREHENSION : DR GLADYS WEST

- How well do you follow instructions and listen?
- Work in groups of four (4).
- Choose a reader.
- Have him/or her read aloud.
- Raise your hand to answer the questions that follow.
- Then, reread the story to yourself.

Dr. Gladys West- A Woman of Direction

Have you ever been travelling, and got completely lost? Have you in the past gone on a trip with your family and they thought they knew where they were going? Then, it turned out that they did not have a clue because you ended up parked in a meadow instead of the parking lot of a mall. Suddenly, the person who was so confident, that they did not need to stop and ask for directions becomes extremely bewildered as to their current location and has no idea whether to proceed to the right or to the left. The smart one usually breaks the wall of confusion by volunteering to use the Global Positioning System (GPS).

Gladys Mae Brown, a black woman, is the inventor of the GPS. She was born in rural Virginia on October 27, 1930. Her life began uneventfully, but as she aged she demonstrated an aptitude or natural ability for mathematics. She thus pursued a first degree and then a master's degree in the same subject. She worked as a mathematician on the U.S. Naval Proving Ground which is a weapons laboratory. While there, she met her husband, Ira V. West, another black mathematician. They got married and had three children.

Gladys West was a project manager at a company that was the first to show that satellites could be used to observe oceanographic statistics and other pertinent information. Due to her work, a satellite was programmed to create computer models of Earth's surface. The project was called GEOSAT. West along with her team created a program that could accurately calculate the orbits of satellites. This is merely the path that an object takes around another object due to gravity. From these calculations the exact shape of Earth could be determined. This was known as a model of Earth called a geoid. This model, along with later updates enabled the GPS system to make accurate calculations of any place on Earth.

Like NASA black female mathematicians in the movie, "Hidden Figures" West too is one such figure whose significant role in contributing to science went unrecognized due to her gender and race. West, what a fitting surname for someone who made the GPS. Unrecognized no more for her contributions to science and technology. Would you not concur?

1. State three facts heard about Gladys West.

____

____

____

2. What does GPS stand for? ______________________________

____

3. What is the model of Earth called? ______________________________

____

4. Define an orbit. ______________________________

____

____

5. Explain the meaning of the movie titled, "Hidden Figures." ______________________________

____

____

____

____

____

____

6. What literary device is used in the title, "Hidden Figures?"

7. Name and explain the literary device that is used in the title of text.

WRITING A BIOGRAPHY REPORT : WILLIAM ROBINSON CLARKE

Biography means, "life writing." Biographies are typically about famous people and it is an account of someone's life written by someone else. Biographies entail information about the subject's childhood, education, work, coming- of- age events, relationships, failures, successes and death in order to create a well-rounded description of the subject.

When writing a biography these are the fundamental questions that must be answered in order to make a meaningful read:

- Did they change their world?
- Did the world change them?
- Did they transcend/transform the time in which they lived?
- Why or why not? And how?

A thesis statement must be in the first paragraph of The Biography. The thesis statement is the GPS of your essay. It tells the reader the three main points that you will be discussing throughout the essay. The thesis statement is the last sentence in the first paragraph.

Format for Writing a Biography

1. ***Paragraph 1***- Introduce the pilot. Information should include full name, date of birth, place of birth, schooling, family information such as number of children, wife, name of parents. Create a thesis statement before proceeding to next paragraph.

2. ***Paragraph 2***- Share how he contributed to history and changed the world. What did he do? Highlight the activities that he engaged in to warrant him a place in history.

3. ***Paragraph 3***- Write the obstacles or hardships he endured and encountered but overcame them all.

4. ***Paragraph 4***- Outline the accolades, awards, certificates he received due to his contributions.

5. ***Paragraph 5***- Conclusion of report should state the most interesting information you learnt and why the reader should research the pilot further.

Edit the information and then transfer it to create one of the following:

- A pamphlet
- A brochure
- A mini-book
- A lapbook

Do include a photograph of the pilot.

Remember, a biography is a literary genre that is loyal to facts, so please do the necessary research. Do begin!

First Jamaican Black Combat Pilot, William Robinson Clarke

The self-taught engineer- Retrieved from https://www.engadget.com/2015-02-20-jerry-lawson-game-pioneer.html

READING TECHNIQUES- SKIMMING AND SCANNING : JERRY LAWSON

Skimming is reading quickly to get an overview of what the text is saying and to look for general information. As you skim, you may see the main idea, but not all the details. Consequently, your comprehension of text will be lower. When skimming do the following:

- Read the title.
- Read the caption.
- Read headings and subheadings.
- Read the first and last sentence of each paragraph.

Scanning is also reading quickly, but the intention is to find or locate information for specific answers. When scanning do the following:

- Look at the text section by section.
- Focus on the nouns and verbs in each sentence.
- Look for bold or repetitive terms.
- Look for lists.

Jerry Lawson- The Video Game Pioneer

Gerald Anderson Lawson was born on December 1, 1940. He was the first African American engineer who made an impact in the computing beginnings of the video game era.

The 21st century gamer may find it difficult to imagine a gamer in the early 1970s, when most electronic games were only available on mainframe computers in university labs. However, Lawson while in his garage, programmed and used his own Digital Equipment Corporation PDP-8 minicomputer to create a game. It was based on the space-themed, text only game Lunar Lander.

He developed the first cartridge-based home video game console system. He was thus dubbed by Black Enterprise magazine as the "father of the videogame cartridge." In the mid- 1970s he helped to create the Fairchild Channel F. This is a home entertainment machine. Due to his contributions, he paved the way for systems such as Atari 2600, Nintendo Xbox and PlayStation. (Biography.com Editors,2020).

His contributions has earned him a permanent spot that is on display at The World Video Game Hall at The Strong National Museum of Play in Rochester, New York. His groundbreaking technology paved the way for modern gaming and he was black.

1. Which paragraph states what Lawson first developed?

2. Name one (1) contribution he has made to the "gaming society"

3. Where did Lawson first build a minicomputer?

4. In four (4) sentences write the summary of the passage.

5. In your own words, define "groundbreaking technology" based on how it is used in the passage.

6. What does it mean to be self-taught?

USING PROJECT BASED LEARNING TO BUILD COMPREHENSION, LITERACY AND RESEARCH SKILLS.

Did you know that there are Jamaican inventors who have made significant contributions to various fields both locally and internationally? Here is a list:

- Dr. Thomas Phillip Lecky
- Robert Rashford
- Dr. Lawrence Williams
- Austin James Thomas
- Dr. Manley West
- Dr. David Daniel Phillips
- Dr. Paula Tennant
- Joel Sadler
- Dr. Henry Lowe

In single-gender groups of five (5) choose one of the inventors stated above to research and present to the class. Each group member must be assigned a specific task to showcase the chosen Jamaican inventor. Do not forget to:

1. Communicate
2. Collaborate
3. Critically think and
4. Create a winning presentation as a team!

Here is the list of assigned tasks for each group member:

- **Group member 1**: Present by sharing background information about inventor.
- **Group member 2**: Present information about what was invented and its use/s.
- **Group member 3**: Present on how the invention has helped Jamaica and/or the world.
- **Group member 4**: Present through the display of a diagram, picture or a video the invention, while explaining how it works or operates.

- **Group member 5**: Summarize the key or most important or salient points of the presentation.

A list of a few skills needed for effective research:

- Summarizing
- Paraphrasing
- Skimming
- Scanning
- Selecting
- Using citations accurately

If your gender number in class does not facilitate single-sex grouping, do engage in this activity how it is possible. In addition, Wikipedia is not a credible source to retrieve information, so use other reputable websites. Cite references used as is observed to the back of this workbook. *Use the APA format. The Purdue Owl Online Writing Lab can show you how to write any citation correctly using the most updated format. When citing sources, list in alphabetical order.

How to Cite References:

Example 1

- An online article:

Alexander, K.L. (2019). *Mae Jemison.* Retrieved from https://www.womenshistory.org/education-resources/biographies/mae-jemison

(last name of author, their initials. (year of article). Title of article. Retrieved from link of article/url)

Example 2

- A book:

Feldman, S. R & Landry O. (2012). *Discovering the lifespan: Canadian ed.* United States of America: Pearson Education.

(authors. (year of publication). Title of book. Country: Name of Publisher.

Please note, when writing titles of books, articles, blogs or wherever information is retrieved from, ONLY capitalize the first letter of title. However, if the title consists of PROPER NOUNS, do begin each word with a capital letter. Italicize titles.

Example 3:

Write the reference when information is retrieved from YouTube:

Example 4:

Write the reference when information is retrieved from a blog:

THE TEACHER'S GUIDE - GOALS AND OBJECTIVES

INTRODUCTION

A topic such as Global Black History requires more than one discipline to gain a deeper insight and understanding for attaining intellectual competence and comprehension. Multiple perspectives have to be presented on this issue so as to grasp the complexity and necessity of including this in the curriculum as black representation empowers and includes the learner in the teaching/ learning process by showcasing models that look like them, have overcome obstacles that they are currently facing, have transformed history and have played an integral role in the development of the society that they currently live in.

Learning is thus not perceived as being done in isolation but rather an interconnectedness that synthesizes and analyzes for the accumulation of varying concepts centered around one central theme. The learner will demonstrate comprehension of a passage through the different types of questions that must be answered at the literal, inferential (interpretive) and evaluative level while honing literacy skills which incorporate, reading, writing, listening and speaking.

Global Black History is a coherent and coordinated whole that will answer the following questions:

- How is Global Black History necessary as a Jamaican who resides in a global community?
- What is the interrelationship between Global Black History and issues that teenagers struggle with such as: self-concept, self-worth, self-value, and self-esteem?
- What is the correlation between Global Black History and IDENTITY, ETHNICITY OR RACE?

A curriculum needs to cater to the leaners' needs based on their current developmental stage emotionally, socially, psychologically, intellectually and most definitely spiritually while simultaneously fostering 21st century skills such as media, information and technology literacy. The comprehension of how to evaluate and use effectively the information presented and ascertain its validity and credibility takes comprehension a step further beyond the traditional text as the only means to answer literal, inferential and evaluative questions.

Through Global Black History, learning thus becomes relatable as social - emotional connections can be made and hence deepen comprehension, retention and expression. A curriculum that does not truly answer the question "Who am I?" educates a society to respond, "Why should I care?"

The teenager is struggling to find SELF. Thus, it is of utmost importance that the curriculum reflects teaching and learning that aids in the discovery and development of SELF-IDENTITY. Is our curriculum effectively building a confident Jamaican who is self-aware of their ethnicity, their roots and fostering a love for their colour? Global Black History is a beginning to the holistic development of teenagers who are struggling to find themselves in this world by exposing them to concepts that promote growth not just academically, but emotionally, socially, psychologically, and undoubtedly spiritually. There is a strong correlation between IDENTITY and ETHNICITY. When a teenager grasps this, then they learn to love their RACE, which has a ripple effect in fostering PATRIOTISM.

How The Interdisciplinary Approach may be used in the classroom.

The Interdisciplinary Approach encourages and facilitates team teaching or collaborative teaching. For example, the first topic, Context Clues provides The English Language teacher with the opportunity to **engage learners**. To introduce the topic, **The English Language Teacher** may have learners focus on the word "umber" below image and use visual cues to decipher its meaning. An **explanation** of the topic and a discussion of the image may then ensue. The text is then read.

As learners become familiar with its content, **The History Teacher** can **elaborate** or provide additional details for more increased background knowledge about ancient Egyptians. In addition, **The Social Studies Teacher** can show the places mentioned in passage so as to explore regions such as Africa, Israel and Egypt on The World Map. **The Religious Education Teacher** may then expound or share more about Solomon, the scriptures highlighted and the "exodus" of Israelite slaves from Egypt. This methodology empowers global connections to text and provides a more holistic teaching/learning experience. Applying this methodology, deepens comprehension for learners, while building better relationships with their teachers. Teachers, you are modelling cooperation and team work (hidden curriculum). Learners will thus have more opportunities to use multiple resources, materials and not just the workbook for more meaningful associations to experience increased learning and understanding of text for the development of self-identity. The **evaluative** methodologies are thus more effective. While this approach may not always be possible, when the opportunity arises, do employ it.

THE INTERDISCIPLINARY CURRICULUM APPROACH AND DESIGN TO INCREASE COMPREHENSION, LITERACY AND RESEARCH SKILLS IN GLOBAL BLACK HISTORY

Vision Statement: Building self-awareness of identity so as to assimilate as productive citizens in a global economy.

Mission Statement: Increasing comprehension, literacy and research skills in Global Black History using an Interdisciplinary Design Approach.

Purpose: The goals/ objectives of this framework must be used in tangent with the Building Comprehension and Literacy Skills in Global Black History workbook to effectively build knowledge and understanding of key concepts that provide practice and development in critical thinking skills and global concepts that extend beyond the four walls of a classroom. Through the interdisciplinary approach 21st century skills are fostered such as problem-solving, creativity, collaboration and communication.

Each topic lends itself to differentiated instruction, formative assessment or graded work.

Goals/Aims

1. To expose learners to content that is relevant to their history, age and gender.
2. To foster creation and innovation and promote entrepreneurial thinking.
3. To see the inter- relatability between textbook knowledge and the real world.
4. To arouse interest to learn more, be open minded, be an independent thinker who learns not just to regurgitate content, but to write and listen critically.
5. To grasp their role in the group dynamics or setting.
6. To develop a greater awareness of their identity at home, school, church and the wider community that extends to the global hemisphere.
7. To promote the comprehension strategy of questioning and so gain practice in oral communication skills.

8. To foster integrative thinking through discussions and presentations in Global Black History.

9. To increase knowledge in Religious Education, Social Studies, Civics, History, English Language, English Literature, and Literacy to comprehend Global Black History, and so realize that learning is interrelated and not isolated.

10. To be cognizant of terminologies such as: self-concept, self-esteem and identity formation so as to know their place in the global economy.

11. To accomplish identity achievement.

12. To attain psychological health, achievement motivation and moral reasoning.

13. To appreciate their ethnicity and thus embrace the colour of their skin.

14. To build awareness of the accomplishments of black people outside of Jamaica and so break cultural ignorance barriers.

15. To possess appropriate role models that are a representation of their race.

16. To engage in activities that require different use and types of skills and abilities.

17. To prepare for the global community that thrives on knowledge not just for intellectual growth but for social interactions.

18. To perceive themselves as valuable members in Jamaica within a global community and understand the inter-connectedness of their roles in the world at large.

19. To expose learners to content that is relevant to their history, developmental stage and gender.

20. To understand the spiritual ramifications of not knowing one's identity.

21. To use Global Black History content to promote morals, values, patriotism, love for mankind and their environment.

22. To foster higher engagement in the teaching/learning process.

23. To highlight the learners' strengths and interests as content is pulled from a variety of disciplines and so the synthesis of ideas/concepts is organic, thus accumulation and retention of ideas are greater.

24. To provide an intrinsic motivation to acquire new knowledge.

25. To truly understand a cultural assimilation model- the melting pot - "Out

of many, One People."

26. To foster the desire to research for both personal and academia purposes.

27. To educate learners on how to cite sources accurately using the APA format, whilst in current academic setting and in preparation for higher learning or education.

A Framework for The Interdisciplinary Curriculum Approach to increase **Comprehension**, **Literacy** and **Research Skills** in **GLOBAL BLACK HISTORY.**

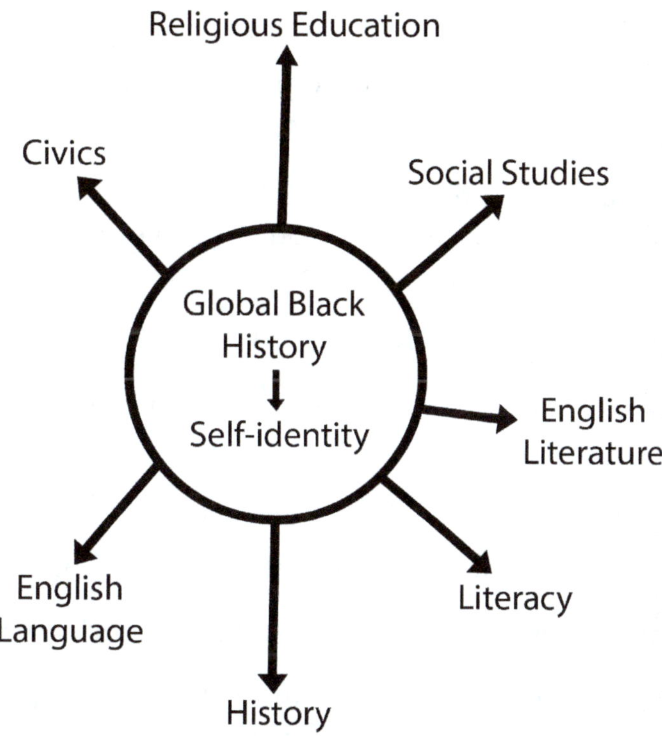

Resource:

DISCIPLINE: RELIGIOUS EDUCATION

Theme: Development of Self-Identity

Topic: Global Black History

Strand: Recognizing and acknowledging the correlation between faith and identity.

Key skills: self- concept and self-esteem development, spiritual awareness and identity, spiritual connection to God (Yahweh), knowledge of scriptures, interpreting scriptures through analysis.

Purpose (Learner Objectives):

1. To grasp a deeper understanding of how to develop emotionally and spiritually.
2. Be motivated to discover their identity in Jesus Christ.
3. See the significance of following Christ over religion.
4. Develop comprehension and literacy skills in scriptures.
5. Analyze bible characters to ascertain and determine that The Bible speaks about ndividuals that are of their skin tone.
6. Develop critical thinking skills through scriptures (analysis, synthesis, inferencing)
7. Read bible for pleasure and research to uncover more black history truths.
8. See their ancestry through scriptures.
9. Develop a more accurate representation of Jesus when visualized.
10. Ascertain through analysis that not everything that media posts/shares/ highlights is factual about the Christian faith.
11. Research to know more about their history hidden in the pages of The Bible.
12. Grow more confident in their Christian faith.

DISCIPLINE: CIVICS

Theme: Promoting Patriotism through the development of self-identity.

Topic: Global Black History

Strand: Fostering love for country and the colour of skin through self- identity acceptance.

Key skills: Developing self- awareness of their role in the global community, fostering love and loyalty to country through research and knowledge content, deepening understanding of motto, pride in skin tone and citizenship, understanding role of an activist

Purpose (Learner Objectives):

1. To instill leadership qualities and skills.
2. To develop patriotism through exposure to new, relevant and relatable content.
3. To build and encourage love for country and self through black representation.
4. To foster compassion for fellow black brothers and sisters.
5. To impart the necessity to take initiative to solve problems in country and globally.
6. To understand that their role as a citizen not just in Jamaica, but also globally.
7. To foster a social activist mindset by introducing terms and situations that showcase injustice, inequality and the need to respond peacefully and speak up respectfully about issues that demonstrate unfairness.
8. Recognize that the Civil Rights movement was a global occurrence.
9. Discuss the political parties' views as it relates to independence and fashion.
10. Be an advocate for change and progress and thus lead by example.

DISCIPLINE: HISTORY AND GEOGRAPHY

Theme: Development of Self- Concept and Identity through Ancestry.

Topic: Global Black History

Discipline: History and Geography

Strand: Building self-esteem through the understanding and explaining of black genealogy.

Key Skills: building awareness of self through knowledge about their ancestors, understand and visualize societies of the past, develop self-identity through historical facts, learn about the values and morals their ancestors possessed, teaching past mistakes of ancestors, connect events together to become a more rounded person, advance in an understanding of the world and current events.

Purpose (Learner Objectives):

1. Be familiar with cardinal points for unearthing locations in the prescribed "historical context".
2. Become aware of topographical changes and demarcations that may have transformed throughout history and alter the world as we presently see it.
3. Promote high self-esteem through content about ancestry.
4. Appreciate the contributions their enslaved ancestors made to their free present.
5. Connect their history and genealogy to the people in The Bible.
6. Understand that history is not limited to ONLY the colonial perspective.
7. Stimulate interest to learn more about their past.
8. Grasp the history of why being black is something to celebrate and be proud of.
9. Though the interdisciplinary approach grasp a deeper and more thorough understanding of their history.
10. See the scientific, technological, medical, religious and economic

achievements that blacks have accomplished throughout history.

11. Desire to "make history" and leave a legacy of black greatness.

12. Study the continent of Africa and the country of Israel.

13. Envisioning themselves in the world as they peruse the World Map. (global citizen)

14. See through concrete representations, explanations and exploring of World Map where their ancestors came from.

DISCIPLINE: SOCIAL STUDIES- SOCIAL SKILLS, ETHICS, PHILOSOPHY, PSYCHOLOGY AND ANTHROPOLOGY PERSPECTIVE FOR SOCIAL -EMOTIONAL DEVELOPMENT.

Theme: Demonstrate a clear awareness of emotions, attitudes and norms that are deemed appropriate for growth in self-identity.

Topic: Global Black History

Strand: Fostering ethical behavior changes through belief in faith and behaviour modification suggestions through text.

Key Skills: Making logical decisions, Treating others fairly without prejudice, demonstrate love towards mankind

Purpose (Learner Objectives):

1. Make connections to mindset and negative attitudes to lack of self-esteem and identity and work to improve it.
2. Change psyche or thought process to view their classmates as individuals to show forgiveness and kindness to.
3. Increase in morality in modes of conduct mentally and physically.
4. Assess their obligations, rights and deem what is morally acceptable or unacceptable based on societal expectations (difference between right and wrong)
5. Formulate basic ideas about the Christian faith, its truth and meaning.
6. Grasp through logical thinking and reasoning that there is a God.
7. Debunk the evolution theory.
8. See the correlation, relationship and similarities between past ancestors' cultures and current ideas, customs and social behavior.
9. Forgive actions committed to ancestors by slave owners.
10. Use knowledge presented to become more loving, selfless, respectful, compassionate, diligent and empathetic.

11. Affirm their identity with power and conviction.

12. To note that their ancestors had a family unit that loved each other.

13. Improve communication skills as they listen and respond to each other in group settings and collaborate to complete a shared goal.

14. Experience more meaningful bonding experiences through interactions, shared ideas and information.

15. Interact to prepare for professional relationships.

16. Handle disagreements respectfully while enhancing problem-solving skills.

17. Develop leadership roles and skills.

DISCIPLINE: SOCIAL STUDIES- GLOBAL CONNECTIONS

Theme: Promoting participatory skills to increase self-identity as a Jamaican citizen in a global community.

Topic: Global Black History

Strand: Developing Self-Identity as a Global Citizen.

Key Skills: fostering both civic local/global compassion and love, developing community and collaboration, heightening cross-cultural awareness, appreciating diversity, promoting and accepting inclusion, celebrating differences.

Purpose (Learner Objectives):

1. Evaluate their role as a Jamaican in a global community.
2. Explain the significance of The National Pledge.
3. Recite the National Anthem.
4. Analyze their part to play as a Jamaican to develop their country.
5. Define the term "patriotism"
6. Recognize the significance of their input to innovate for social development.
7. See the interconnectedness of how global past social events have impacted their free social present.
8. Ascertain how political parties have influenced fashion.
9. Note how social activism can bring about social change both locally and globally.
10. Recognize their role as social beings to impact society positively through innovation, creativity and collaboration.
11. Envision their role as a citizen of the world and thus take the relevant social, environmental and economic actions.

DISCIPLINE: ENGLISH LANGUAGE AND ENGLISH LITERATURE

Theme: Using comprehension strategies to aid self-identity development.

Topic: Global Black History

Strand: Honing self-identity development through varying comprehension strategies and genres of writings.

Key Skills: reading and analyzing various texts about global black history, understanding comprehension strategies, applying definitions of comprehension terms to increase understanding of texts, answering questions, writing responses, improving critical thinking and reasoning, increasing logical thinking skills.

Purpose (Learner Objectives):

1. Answer questions at the literal, inferential and evaluative level.
2. Apply definitions of comprehension terminologies to answer questions with a high degree of accuracy.
3. Foster the improvement of reading and writing skills.
4. Promote the improvement of reading and writing skills.
5. See the correlation between the disciplines English Language And English Literature.
6. Gain a high degree of competence in analyzing and synthesizing information for academic advancement.
7. Increase confidence in critical thinking.
8. Foster enjoyment and engagement in reading as texts are relevant and relatable.
9. Gain tools through comprehension strategies to write and excel at the CSEC level for English Language and English Literature.10.

10. Deepen understanding of Global Black History through English Language and English Literature.

11. Be able to differentiate between fact and opinion.

12. Grasp what it means to infer.

13. Use correct terminologies to compare and contrast.

14. State and define the elements of a short story.

15. Become familiar with and be able to define terms such as: Text-to-Self, Text-To-Text and Text-to-World.

16. Derive deeper meaning from text through Self-Questioning.

17. Employ techniques such as: Foreshadowing, Flashback, Figurative Language, Transitions, Rhetorical Questions, Tone and Mood to enhance and develop their own writing style.

18. Deepen their understanding of research and HOW to research effectively.

19. Make social- emotional connections to passages so their intellect as well as their spirit is fed.

20. Use characterization to improve the writing process.

21. Recognize differences between bias and perspective.

22. Use appropriate techniques to construct an argumentative essay.

23. Follow example provided and create an argumentative essay.

24. Observe and use the types of characters to build interesting stories.

25. Improve paraphrasing and summarizing skills.

26. Employ the use of chronological order and sequencing of events for both plot development and interest.

27. Determine the author's purpose and apply this concept for increasing reading comprehension and knowledge.

28. Research and cite sources accurately for project based oral presentation.

29. Use research skills to choose relevant information from different types of writing materials for group projects and individual assignments.

DISCIPLINE: LITERACY

Theme: Using Literacy skills (reading, writing, listening, speaking) and concepts in Global Black History to affirm self-identity.

Topic: Global Black History

Strand: Building Literacy Skills in Global Black History.

Key Skills: reading varying genres of writings, writing essays, responding to different types (literal, inferential, evaluative) of questions in both the written and oral format, listening attentively to grasp meaning of texts, employing the use of reading techniques to comprehend passage to answer questions, using reading strategies to research effectively, reading the creole, reading to comprehend how their self-identity is connected to Global Black History.

Purpose (Learner Objectives):

1. Preparing students to read, write, listen and speak more effectively.
2. Watching a movie to prompt dialogue through discussions.
3. Reading and reciting The National Pledge to spark critical thinking and debating skills.
4. Listening to music to arouse emotions that must be described.
5. Building literacy skills across the curriculum to increase retention and engagement.
6. Using literacy to make connections in learning to develop and expand writing and speaking vocabulary.
7. Increase fluency and comprehension abilities as passages are read.
8. Facilitate the growth of both content area reading and disciplinary reading.
9. Intertwine content area reading and disciplinary reading for a more comprehensive understanding of Global Black History.
10. Encourage open-ended questioning about Global Black History through

the interdisciplinary approach.

11. Gaining competence in creative writing, reading, expression skills, digital and media literacy skills.

12. Translating and writing the dialect/patois in Standard Jamaican English (SJE)

SUMMARY

The Interdisciplinary instruction design functions as a framework to foster learning that puts aside preconceived notions to develop a thorough understanding of Global Black History through varying disciplines to answer complex and topical issues.

Each discipline seeks to answer questions independently, yet through an integration of content. This lessens misunderstanding of concepts and puts the learner at an advantage to gain and retain more knowledge.

Educational researchers have identified a number of educational benefits for learners when interdisciplinary learning is applied. They are:

- Recognize bias
- Think critically
- Tolerate ambiguity
- Acknowledge and appreciate ethical concerns (Kavaloski 1979, Newell 1990, Field et al, 1994)

According to the National Council for Teachers of English, "educational experiences are more authentic and of greater value to students when the curricula reflects real life which is multi-faceted rather than being compartmentalized into neat subject-matter packages. In other words, world problems are complex and so no single discipline can adequately describe and resolve these issues." (Edwards 1996, Gaff & Ratclif 1997, Lein 1996).

Through this curriculum the following questions will be answered for both boys and girls:

- Self-Identity- Who am I?
- Self- concept- What am I like?
- Self-esteem- How do I like Myself? Do my successes and achievements define me? (external)
- Self-worth- How do I see Myself? Am I worthy of love? (internal)
- Self- value- Do I respect Myself?

Through using an interdisciplinary curriculum approach, to teach Global Black History, teenagers will go through less of what Erik Erikson, the psychologist, coined as "identity-versus-identity-confusion" stage. They will thus accomplish as another psychologist, James Marcia proposes, a milestone, termed, "identity achievement." (Feldman & Landry, 2012).

ABOUT THE AUTHOR

Kadeen Dobbs has a Bachelor of Education in Language Arts and Spanish. She also has a Diploma in Primary Education with an emphasis in Children's Literature. This has provided her with teaching experience in Reading and being a part of the decision-making process to create a literacy syllabus. Kadeen graduated with Honours from Humber College Institute of Technology and Advanced Learning in Toronto with a Diploma in Early Childhood Education and acquired experience as a Registered Early Childhood Educator at the YMCA. She was also a supervisor for a daycare centre and a coordinator for PLASP, one of Toronto's largest before and after-school programmes.

Kadeen has taught in Canada, The Bahamas and Jamaica. She has done a tutor certification course which she successfully completed while residing in Canada. She has worked as a tutor at The Writing Centre at Humber College and Head Start Learning also in Canada to every class, creed and colour. In addition, as technology has bridged the gap, through her online tutoring services, she has tutored individuals in Jamaica, Canada, Bermuda and The United States of America.

Kadeen is a trained and certified teacher that currently teaches English Language and Literature to learners ages 13-18.

This is her third educational workbook, and Literacy is one of her passions. Her first workbook, "Read, Draw and Write Prompts: For Visual, Auditory, Reading/ Writing, Kinesthetic and Remedial Learners as well as "The Engaged Reader- An Integrated Approach" are presently available on Amazon

REFERENCES

AfroBiz (2019). *The secret meaning of the African cornrows.* Retrieved from https://www.afrobizworld.com/the-secret-meaning-of-the-african-cornrows

Alexander, K.L. (2019) *Mae Jemison.* Retrieved from https://www.womenshistory.org/education-resources/biographies/mae-jemison

Allan. L. (2023) *Strange fruit hanging from a tree.* Retrieved from https://www.austincc.edu/dlauderb/1302/Lyrics/StrangeFruitLyrics1937.htm

As it happens. AP. NEWSROOM. (2022) *Sheryl Lee Ralph, 66,1st-time nominee wins Emmy award.* Retrieved from https://apnews.com/article/emmy-awards-entertainment-sitcoms-tv-172154473a7c2f3278287368780be476

Ashley, M. (2023). *Maurice Ashley International Grandmaster.* Retrieved from https://mauriceashley.com/bio/

Ask Hip Hop. (2023). *DJ Kool here (Clive Campbell).* Retrieved from https://history.hiphop/dj-kool-herc-clive-campbell/

Bible Gateway. (2023). *biblegateway.* Retrieved from https://www.biblegateway.com/

Baird, S.C. (2013). *Why don't dark-skinned people get sunburns?* Retrieved from https://www.wtamu.edu/~cbaird/sq/2013/08/19/why-dont-dark-skinned-people-get-sunburns/

Christ -Centered Mall. (2016). Warner Sallman biography. Retrieved from https://christcenteredmall.com/stores/art/sallman/sallmanbiography.htm

Christian Answers.Net (2021). *Who and what is Cush?* Retrieved from https://christiananswers.net/dictionary/cush.html

Conner, Y. (2020). *Jesus is not white.* Retrieved from https://jude3project.org/blog/jesusisnotwhite

Ducksters. (2022). *Biography Shaka Zulu.* Retrieved from https://www.ducksters.com/history/africa/shaka_zulu.php

Embassy of Jamaica. (n.d.) *History of Jamaica.* Retrieved from https://www.embassyofjamaica.org/about_jamaica/history.htm

ESPN. (2023). *Usain Bolt.* Retrieved from http://en.espn.co.uk/espn/sport/player/1626.html

Feldman, S. R & Landry O. (2012). *Discovering the lifespan. Canadian ed.* United States of America: Pearson Education

Gilchrist, C. (2014, March 16). *Jamaica's first supermodel turns author.* Retrieved from https://jamaica-gleaner.com/gleaner/20140316/ent/ent82.html#google_vignette

Grunge. (2019). *Tragic Things You Never Knew About Bob Marley's Past.* Retrieved from YouTube https://youtu.be/ZeTAGPRfjwo?si=2w3iCwSuiG1xCEDY

History Extra. (2023). *Who was Cleopatra? Her life, her love affairs and her children, plus 6 little-known facts.* Retrieved from https://www.historyextra.com/period/ancient-egypt/cleopatra-facts-ancient-egypt-beauty-life-death-egyptian-roman-caesar/

Holloway, April. (2017). *The braided rapunzels of Namibia: every stage of life is reflected in their hair.* Retrieved from https://www.ancient-origins.net/news-history-ancient-traditions/braided-rapunzels-namibia-every-stage-life-reflected-their-hair-021501#google_vignette

Horne, M. (2019). *A visual history of iconic black hairstyles.* Retrieved from https://www.history.com/news/black-hairstyles-visual-history-in-photos

Hutchinson, J (2021). *They thought they hurt her by saying, "teck dat dutty bumpyhead gyal off di tv."* Retrieved from https://jamaicans.com/they-thought-they-hurt-by-saying-teck-dat-dutty-bumpyhead-gyal-off-di-tv/#google_vignette

It is written. (2020). *It is written-Black Wall Street.* Retrieved from YouTube https://youtu.be/20PnA4f08no?si=QsFGB3GhBziJI4Ts

Jamaica experiences. (2019). *The story of the Jamaican bobsled team.* Retrieved from https://www.jamaicaexperiences.com/blogs/details/article/the-story-of-the-jamaican-bobsled-team

Jamaica Information Service. (2023*). Usain St. Leo Bolt.* Retrieved from https://jis.gov.jm/information/famous-jamaicans/usain-st-leo-bolt/

Jamaica Observer. (2023). *Ms. Sheryl Lee Ralph Jamaica's pride and joy.* Retrieved from https://www.jamaicaobserver.com/editorial/ms-sheryl-lee-ralph-jamaicas-pride-and-joy/

Johnson, R. (2017, July 7). *Althea Laing: The cover girl.* Retrieved from https://www.jamaicaobserver.com/entertainment/althea-laing-the-cover-girl/

Jerry Lawson (engineer) facts for kids. (2023). *Kiddie Encyclopedia.* Retrieved from https://kids.kiddle.co/Jerry_Lawson_(engineer)

Jewish Virtual Library. (2023). *Ancient Jewish History: The Two Kingdoms (c. 920 BCE-597 BCE).* Retrieved from https://www.jewishvirtuallibrary.org/the-two-kingdoms-of-israel4

King, Abby. (n.d.) *Missionaries in Jamaica.* Retrieved from https://scholar.library.miami.edu/emancipation/religion2.htm

Korney,Stephanie. (2021). *Angella Reid, Jamaica-Caribbean- American woman of influence.* Retrieved from https://jamaicans.com/angella-reid-jamaica-caribbean-american-woman-of-influence/

Leon, F. (2018). *How Jesus became widely accepted as being white/unpack that.* Retrieved from https://youtu.be/dfJCyDmTwyg?si=wtJOStN5TNMjWR0l

Lesso, R. (2022*). Were ancient Egyptians black? Let's look at the evidence.* Retrieved from

https://www.thecollector.com/were-ancient-egyptians-black/

Lion Locs. (n.d.) *The history of dreadlocks.* (Blog post). Retrieved from https://lionlocs.com/blogs/dreadlocks/history-of-dreadlocks

Mendel, G. (2013) *DNA Mysteries: The Search For Adam-National Geographic Documentary HD.* Retrieved from YouTube https://youtu.be/gkl37NTHKLU?si=1Mxz82IhONpODdlF

NFL (2023, February 12). *Lift Every Voice and Sing Super Bowl LVII.* Retrieved from YouTube https://youtu.be/p0Qzu6r40_4?si=wkAg2smJ0NK9qjia

Nielsen, A. E. (2015). *Bessie Stringfield (1911-1993).* Retrieved from https://www.blackpast.org/african-american-history/bessie-stringfield-1911-1993/

Nkiti. (2022, May 30). *A Guide To Traditional African Hairstyles And Their Origin* (Blog post). Retrieved from https://nkitidesigns.com/blogs/stories/traditional-african-hairstyles-and-their-origin

Nova online. (2000). *The Lemba, The Black Jews of Southern Africa.* Retrieved from https://www.pbs.org/wgbh/nova/israel/familylemba.html#:~:text=The%20Lemba%2C%20The%20Black%20Jews%20of%20Southern%20Africa&text=This%20Bantu%2Dspeaking%20group%20claimed,and%20Semitic%2Dsounding%20clan%20names

Park, George. (2023). *Animism*. Retrieved from https://www.britannica.com/topic/animism

Roberts, N. (2023). *Claudine Gay becomes first black President of Harvard University*. Retrieved from https://www.bet.com/article/4payps/claudine-gay-first-black-harvard-president-inaugurated

Sparks, K. (2023) *Lester Holt American broadcast journalist and news anchor.* Retrieved from https://www.britannica.com/topic/Lester-Holt

Smith, F. R. (Producer), & Gates Jr., L.H. (Executive Producer). Black History in Two Minutes or So. (YouTube Channel). USA.

Starting Point: Teaching and Learning Economics. (2023). *Why teach with an Interdisciplinary Approach?* Retrieved from https://serc.carleton.edu/econ/interdisciplinary/why.html#:~:text=Interdisciplinary%20instruction%20allows%20us%20to,them%20to%20the%20learning%20process

Tagoe, V.C. (2022). *Story of the suit that represented decolonization.* Retrieved from https://face2faceafrica.com/article/story-of-the-suit-that-represented-decolonization

Taylor, S.M. (2022). *Hidden Black History: 7 African Queens Who Have Made Their Mark.* Retrieved from https://www.ebony.com/7-african-queens-history/#google_vignette

Ted-Ed. (2015). *The Atlantic Slave Trade. What too few textbooks told you-Anthony Hazard.* Retrieved from YouTube https://youtu.be/3NXC4Q_4JVg?si=tY9Xcq5wsxgPhPoY

Television Jamaica (2023, Sept) *Sheryl Lee Ralph gets shocking news during interview/ TVJ Entertainment Report.* Retrieved from YouTube https://youtu.be/5HlBVmMphwA?si=szCOfkpgMucc_79d

The Boxing Historian 206 (2015). *National Geographic Forensic Scientist sculpture Adam as a blackman.* Retrieved from YouTube https://youtu.be/Hz-GVwGsgDg?si=EmK5jLj8JIEmzzY6

The Gleaner. (2014). *Jamaica's first supermodel turns author.* Retrieved fromhttps://jamaica-gleaner.com/gleaner/20140316/ent/ent82.html

The White House Historical Association. (2023). Retrieved from https://www.whitehousehistory.org/questions/who-is-the-chief-usher

The editors of Encyclopaedia Britannica. (2023). Retrieved from https://www.britannica.com/biography/Colin-Powell

The editors of Encyclopaedia Britannica. (2023). *What is cultural appropriation?* Retrieved from https://www.britannica.com/story/what-is-cultural-appropriation

This far by faith. (2023). *Religion in Africa: Common Themes.* Retrieved from https://www.pbs.org/thisfarbyfaith/print/journey1.html#:~:text=A%20very%20few%20Africans%20enslaved,which%20were%20animistic%20in%20nature

www.ingramcontent.com/pod-product-compliance
Lightning Source LLC
LaVergne TN
LVHW080846170826
845678LV00006B/1728

* 9 7 8 9 7 6 6 5 5 1 2 3 0 *